A Handbook of Activities

for

Secondary Social Studies Methods

Darla Mallein
Emporia State University

PEARSON

Boston   New York   San Francisco
Mexico City   Montreal   Toronto   London   Madrid   Munich   Paris
Hong Kong   Singapore   Tokyo   Cape Town   Sydney

ISBN 13: 978-0-205-48959-6
ISBN 10: 0-205-48959-1

Printed in the United States of America

10 9 8 7 6 5 4 3 2 1   10 09 08 07 06

Contents

Contents

Contents

Contents

Preface

When I was working on my doctorate, I took an education psychology class that turned me on to brain-based research and the learning strategies that supported the research. However, while fascinated by the research on how the brain learns, I was frustrated by the professor's "do as I say, not as I do" approach of teaching. Instead of modeling the strategies for us, she stood in the front of the room and lectured to us day after day. I vowed then that when I became a college professor, I would practice what I preach and keep lectures to a minimum and hands-on activities at a maximum.

The activities presented in this handbook are the result of that vow. Rather than lecture to my secondary social studies methods students, I try to engage them with hands-on activities and/or cooperative learning activities that require them to read, react, and reflect on information found in our methods textbook, handouts I provide, or articles they are required to bring to class.

All of the activities in this handbook have been used in my methods classroom, although several of them had to be adapted to fit the format of this handbook. Since a wealth of resources can be found on the worldwideweb, many of the activities are internet-based. In fact, my students are required to compile a Teacher Resource Notebook in which they place hardcopies of the information they find on the internet as well as classroom handouts and assignments. By placing these items in a notebook, they'll have a ton of resources at their fingertips when they student teach or enter their own classroom.

In addition to providing information and resources for the beginning social studies teacher, another purpose of this activity handbook is to model strategies or activities that can be used in any classroom. For example, I use a lot of graphic organizers in my classes, so many of those have been included in the handbook as well as some of my favorite strategies like PMI and 3-2-1. I hope all preservice teachers will be able to see beyond the printed page and imagine how they can adapt the activities that appear in this handbook to their own future classrooms.

If you have any questions or comments about the activities in this handbook, please email me (dmallein@emporia.edu). I'd love to hear from you and answer any questions you might have. I hope you enjoy the activities in the handbook.

About the Author

Currently I am the director of the secondary social sciences education program at Emporia State University. As the director, I am responsible for teaching the Intro to Teaching Secondary Social Sciences and the Teaching Secondary and Middle Level Social Sciences Methods courses. I also advise all secondary social sciences majors, supervise student teachers in the field, and direct the Master of Arts in Teaching Social Sciences degree program.

Prior to teaching the secondary social studies methods courses at ESU, I was a classroom teacher for twenty years. I like to share with my preservice teachers that I had a horrible first year of teaching. I think I made every mistake in the book, including using way too many worksheets. In fact, my students nicknamed me "Mrs. Ditto" because I worksheeted them to death. However, one day as I looked up from one of those worksheets we were grading in class and saw the dull, glazed looks on their faces, I decided it was time for **me** to change. Thus, I started using cooperative learning and lots of hands-on projects which prompted some of my students to start calling me "the Project Queen." I didn't mind this nickname, though, and realized that teaching was a lot more fun when my students were engaged in their learning. I still believe that as a college professor.

During the twenty years I was in the public schools, I taught English and social studies in grades 7-12, with the last thirteen years spent teaching 8th grade American history at Emporia Middle School. During my tenure at EMS, I was the lucky recipient of fourteen classroom grants that I used to purchase costumes and other types of materials to bring history to life for my students. In 1997, I was named a Kansas Master Teacher by Emporia State University, and in 1998, I was selected the Kansas Teacher of the Year and one of four finalists for National Teacher of the Year. What a difference my transformation from Mrs. Ditto to the Project Queen had made in my teaching career, and all because I changed my teaching approach from teacher-centered to student-centered!

My educational background includes a Bachelor of Science in Education and a Master of Science degree from Emporia State University and a Ph.D. from Kansas State University. I've been at Emporia State since 2001 and can be reached via email at dmallein@emporia.edu

Acknowledgments

Many thanks to...

Dr. Ellen Hansen, geography professor at Emporia State University, who encouraged me to contact Allyn and Bacon to see if they would be interested in the activities I had created for my methods courses. Without her prodding, I doubt I would have pursued the possibility of creating a handbook of my favorite activities.

Dr. John Sacher, the best department chair I've ever worked for, as well as a good friend and colleague. His encouragement and support will always be appreciated.

my preservice teachers at ESU who inspire me every day to practice what I preach!

my family who has to put up with me when I immerse myself in a project and get stressed out at deadline time.

my best friend Laura who's always there when I need her.

my personal cheerleaders, the Fashionistas aka Daphne, Deb, Heather, Jennie, Kelly, Lisa, and Sandy.

Angela and Tracy at Allyn and Bacon.

Special thanks to my friend and very talented artist, Kelly McLarnon, who designed my Section divider pages. Without Kelly's help, my divider pages would have been very, very plain!

Topaz Design
kelly@kellymclarnon.com

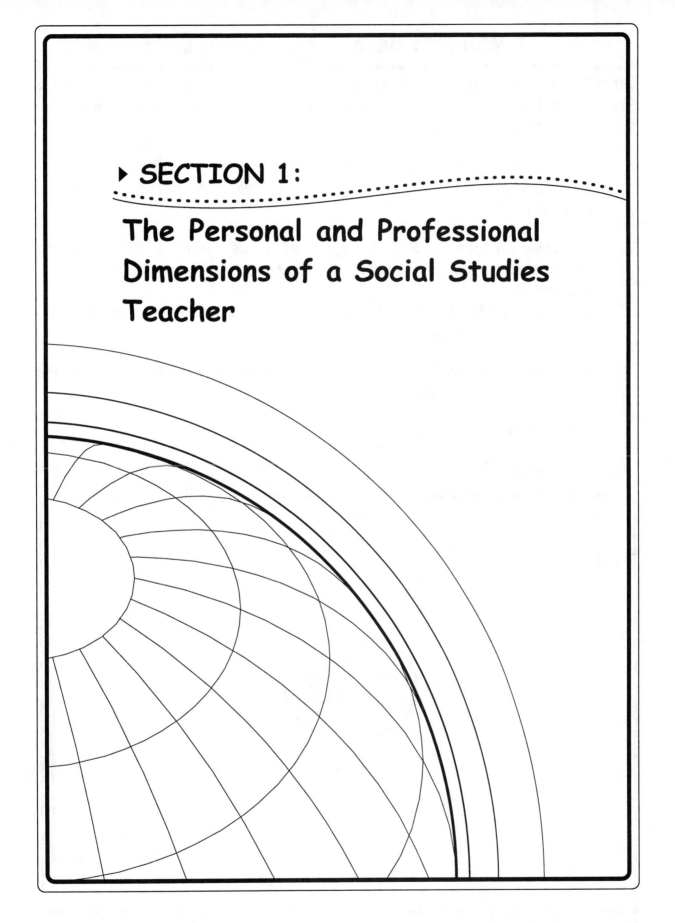

▶ SECTION 1:

The Personal and Professional Dimensions of a Social Studies Teacher

Why I Want to be a Social Studies Teacher

Directions: Brainstorm a list of reasons of why you want to become a Social Studies Teacher by following the steps below to create a Mind Map. Draw your Mind Map on a sheet of white paper.

1)   In the center of the page, write the topic of the Mind Map: "Why I Want to Be a Social Studies Teacher," and then draw a symbol that represents the main topic.

2)   Branching out from the central image, draw images or symbols that represent the reasons you want to be a social studies teacher. (These are your subtopics.)

      a.   Connect the images and symbols with lines or arrows to your central image and/or each other.

      b.   Be sure to label the images and symbols with key words or phrases. Put these key words on the lines.

      c.   Use lots of color!

3)   Be creative!

> *Why I want to be a social studies teacher*

The Ideal Social Studies Teacher

Directions: What characteristics and skills do you think a GREAT (successful) teacher possesses? Fill in the blanks below with words or phrases that describe your image of the Ideal Social Studies Teacher. You are welcome to decorate your successful teacher figure however you wish. When finished, you should have at least EIGHT qualities/skills/personal characteristics. Don't forget to write a summary statement at the bottom of the page.

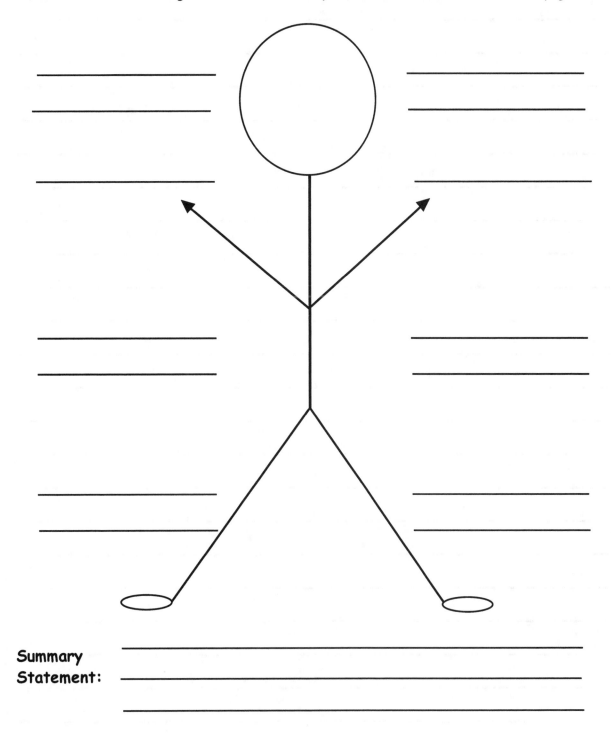

Summary Statement: _____

_____

_____

Essay: My Future Social Studies Classroom

Directions: Write an essay that describes what your future social studies classroom will "look" like. In other words, if a principal or parents were to walk into your classroom unannounced, what would they see? What would your room look like? What would the students be doing? What would you be doing?

_____

_____

_____

_____

_____

_____

_____

_____

_____

_____

_____

_____

_____

_____

_____

_____

_____

_____

Creating a Teacher Resource Notebook

To help you organize the valuable resources you will collect while completing the activities in this handbook (as well as during your education courses), it would be beneficial for you to create a Teacher Resource Notebook in which to place these items.

Directions:

1) **Purchase a 3-ring binder,** preferably one that is called a view binder because it contains a plastic "sleeve" in which you can slip a cover page.

2) **Create a title page for your notebook.**

   a. Include your name and a creative title for the notebook.

   b. Add an inspirational quote that reflects either your teaching philosophy or YOU to your title page.

   c. Place this page on the front of the notebook or as the first inside page of the notebook.

3) **Organize the information into different sections.**

   a. Some categories you may wish to consider are Completed Assignments, Lesson Plans, Teaching History Resources, Teaching Geography Resources, Teaching Economics Resources, etc.

   b. Be sure to organize the Teacher Resource Notebook in categories that will be most beneficial to you in the future.

   c. Use TABBED divider pages to separate the various sections and to make finding the resources easier.

Professional Organizations Handbook

Directions: Create a handbook that contains information about the following professional organizations you may wish to join when you are a classroom teacher, or even now as a student pursuing a degree in social studies education. All can be found on the worldwide web.

> American Historical Association (AHA)
> Global Association of Teachers of Economics (GATE)
> National Council for Geographic Education (NCGE)
> National Council for History Education (NCHE)
> National Council for the Social Studies (NCSS)
> Organization of American Historians (OAH)

1) Use the template below to answer questions about each of the following organizations:

   ☐ How can you contact this organization if you wish to join?
   (Provide URL address of website or Mailing/Phone Information)

   ☐ What is the purpose of the organization?

   ☐ How would belonging to this organization benefit a classroom teacher?

   ☐ What professional publications are published by this organization?

   ☐ Is there a state affiliate for this organization? If so, list the contact information (website and/or mailing information) and list at least one benefit for joining this state organization.

2) When finished, you should have...

   a) a separate typed page for each organization for a total of six typed pages.

   b) answers written in complete sentences.

   c) original answers that haven't been copied and pasted from the website into your word processing document.

> # Put your completed "Professional Organizations Handbook" in your Teacher Resource Notebook.

To Join or not to Join?

Directions: After researching the various social sciences-related professional organizations, answer the following questions:

1) What are the benefits of joining a professional organization? Try to list at least three.

_____

_____

_____

_____

_____

_____

2) Of the six professional organizations you researched, which one would you most likely join? Explain your answer.

_____

_____

_____

_____

_____

3) Which one would be your second choice? Explain your answer.

_____

_____

_____

_____

Teacher Licensure/Certification Activity #1

Directions: While the steps to earn a teaching license or certificate vary from state to state, the steps below are typical for many states.

Step One: Your task for this activity is to arrange the steps for earning and renewing licenses that appear below in random order in the correct sequence. Write the steps on the graphic organizer on the next page.

Complete Teacher Education Program by meeting GPA requirements, successfully completing clinical or field-based experience (student teaching/practicum), and other requirements set by college or university.	Demonstrate competency of state-designed performance assessment during first/second year to receive recommendation for Professional 5-year license from State Department of Education.
Receive conditional or initial 2-year license from State Department of Education upon recommendation of accredited institution and passing scores on Pedagogical and Content Assessments (e.g., Praxis II Principles of Teaching and Learning and Specialty Area Tests).	Successfully complete General Education and Pre-Professional Content Area courses.
	Get accepted into Professional Education Preparation Program (Must meet GPA requirements, pass Basic Skills test like PPST, etc.).

Renew Professional License through state's approved Professional Development Plan.

Step Two: How do the steps for licensure or certification in your state compare to steps you recorded on the graphic organizer?

_____

_____

_____

_____

Teacher Licensure/Certification Activity #1

Directions: Arrange the steps for teacher licensure/certification on the opposite page in the correct order below.

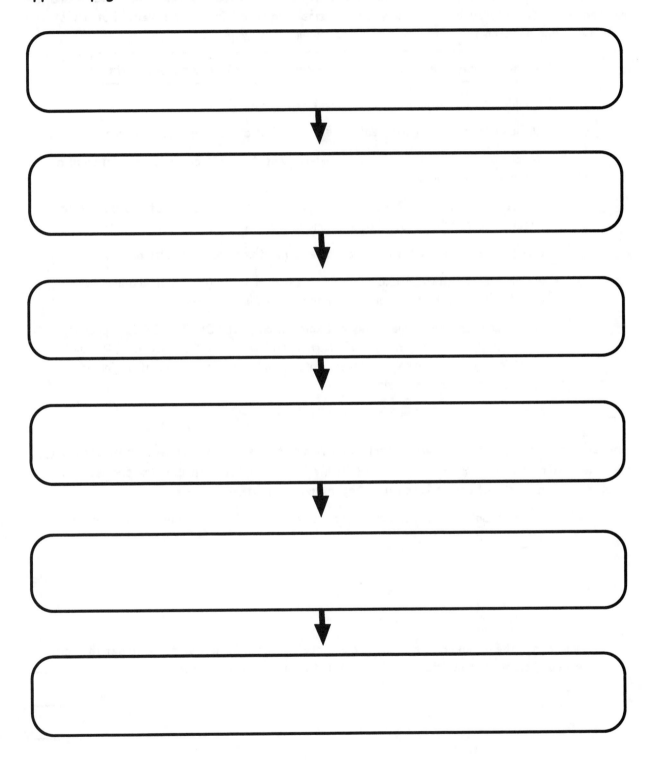

Teacher Licensure/Certification Activity #2

Directions: Access the Teacher Certification Publications website to find the requirements for someone seeking an initial (sometimes called conditional) teaching license/certificate in your state. Scroll through the list of states to find your state and its requirements for licensure. The key for "Items Required" is at the very bottom of the webpage. Put an X on the blank by the items required by your state.

> http://home.earthlink.net/~teachercertification/AtGlance.htm

_____ Completed Application form accompanied by fee of $_____

_____ Official Transcripts (with seal and signature) of all college credits earned

_____ Recommendation of the college or university certifying successful completion of a teacher training program

_____ Copies of personal identification fingerprint cards and/or proof of FBI background check or some other type of background check

_____ Chest X-ray or TB test within past twelve months or other health assessment

_____ Passing Scores on the Praxis I: Pre-Professional Tests (PPST) of Reading, Writing, and Mathematics or other proof of Basic Skills Competency

_____ Official notice of National Teacher Examination (NTE) OR PRAXIS II: Specialty Area Tests including Principles of Learning and Teaching (PLT) scores, OR Praxis III: Classroom Performance Assessments for assessing the skills of beginning teachers in classroom settings.

_____ State-sponsored Testing Program (SSTP)

Answer the following questions with information found on the website above, or by accessing your own state's Department of Education at **www.ksde.org/cert/approvedprogs.html** (Look for heading Certification/Licensure Departments in Other States).

1. What other special requirements will you need to meet before receiving an initial license/certificate in your state?

2. How long is the initial license valid in your state? What do you have to do to get the next level of licensure (some states refer to it as the professional license)?

No Child Left Behind (NCLB) and You

Directions: As a preservice teacher, you need to be aware of the No Child Left Behind Act and how it relates to you as a beginning teacher. Answer the questions below by accessing the United States Department of Education's website (http://www.ed.gov) and clicking on the No Child Left Behind link.

1. When was the No Child Left Behind act passed?

2. On what four principles is NCLB based?

3. According to NCLB, what constitutes a "highly qualified teacher?" How does this correlate with your state's licensure/certification requirements?

4. Why is teacher quality such an important issue?

5. What is your opinion of NCLB's definition of a highly qualified teacher? In other words, do you think its requirements are an accurate measure or indicator of what it takes to be a successful teacher who positively impacts student learning? Explain your answer.

Computers and the Social Studies Teacher

Directions: Give a teacher a computer and internet access, and a wealth of information truly is just a click of the mouse away. Complete the brainstorming activity below by providing as many uses (subtopics) and examples (details) of technology in the social studies classroom as you can think of on the concept web. Feel free to add as many circles and lines as you need.

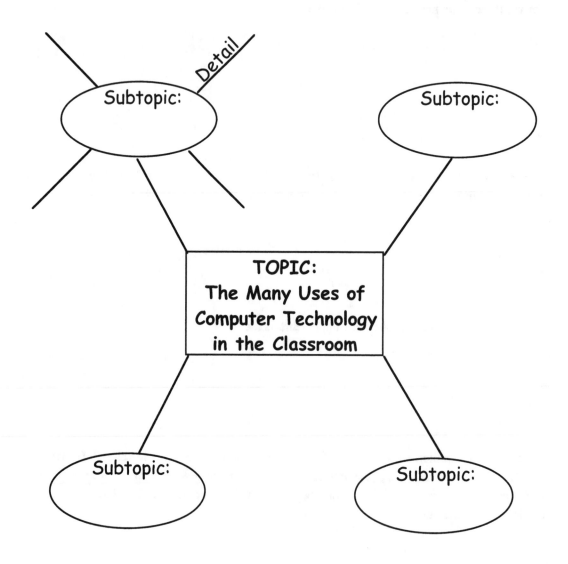

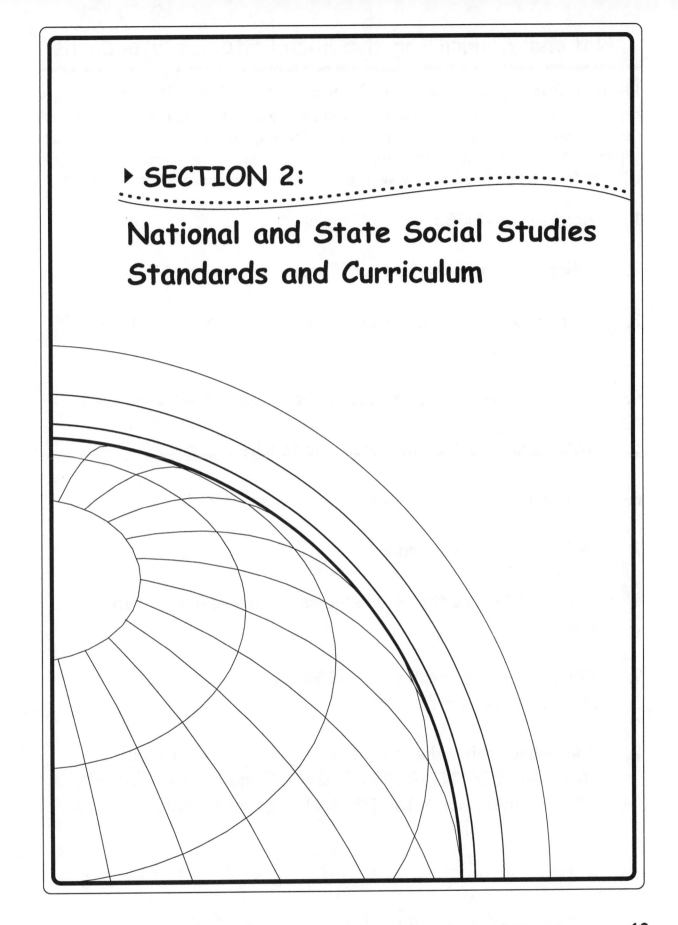

SECTION 2:

National and State Social Studies Standards and Curriculum

National Council for the Social Studies Standards

Directions: Access the National Council for the Social Studies website to answer the questions below. All answers will be found on this page, although you will need to scroll clear down to the bottom of the page to find all of the answers. Write or type your answers to the questions below on another page. Use this URL address for the NCSS website: **www.socialstudies.org/standards/introduction/**

1. According to NCSS, what is "social studies?"

2. What is the primary purpose of social studies?

3. What two main characteristics distinguish social studies as a field of study?

4. What are the three purposes of the social studies standards?

5. What issues do the standards help teachers address?

6. How are the Social Studies Standards organized?

7. Define curriculum standard.

8. How can YOU use the social studies standards in your future classroom?

9. What is the relationship of NCSS's curriculum standards to standards in other fields?

10. Throughout this website page, three "I" words stand out: INTEGRATED, INTERDISCIPLINARY, and INTERRELATED. Why are these words IMPORTANT in social sciences education?

NCSS's Ten Themes of Social Studies Standards

Directions:

1) Access this webpage on NCSS's website:
   www.socialstudies.org/standards/strands/

2) For each of the ten themes listed below:
   a. provide an example of a focus question that would be answered using this theme.
   b. list one course in which this theme could be taught.
   c. draw a symbol that represents that theme.

Example:

I. Culture
   Focus Question: What are the common characteristics of different cultures?
   Course: Anthropology
   Symbol: ┼

NCSS's Ten Themes:

I. Culture

II. Time, Continuity, and Change

III. People, Places, and Environments

IV. Individual Development and Identity

V. Individuals, Groups, and Institutions

VI. Power, Authority, and Governance

VII. Production, Distribution, and Consumption

VIII. Science, Technology, and Society

IX. Global Connections

X. Civic Ideals and Practices

3-2-1 on State Social Studies Standards

Directions:

1.   Access the following website that contains links to all State Departments of Education in the U.S.: **www.ksde.org/cert/approvedprogs.html** Click on your state.

2.   Type "social studies standards" in the search box.

3.   Explore the information in the search results to complete the 3-2-1 activity below.

---

3 Things I found out about my state's social studies standards

2 Resources I found that I can use in my future classroom

1 Question I still have about social studies standards

Social Studies Scope and Sequence Activity

 **Directions:** Look at the sample K-12 Social Studies Scope and Sequence below and then answer the questions at the bottom of the page.

Sample K-12 Social Studies Scope and Sequence:

K - Self
1 - Families
2 - Then and Now
3 - Communities (local history)
4 - State History, Regions of U.S.
5 - U.S. History (Beginnings to 1800)
6 - World history, Geography (less emphasis on chronological approach)
7 - World History, Geography (with emphasis on chronological approach)
8 - U.S. History (1800-1900)
9 - Civics
10 - World/Global history (more emphasis on chronological than regional or cultural approach)
11 - U.S. History (1900 to present)
12 - Government, Economics, electives in Psychology and Sociology

1. How does this sample Social Studies Scope and Sequence compare to...
   A. your own personal K-12 experiences?

   b. the scope and sequence recommended by your state?

2. What are the pros and cons of the sample Social Studies Scope and Sequence provided on this page?

The Debates over Teaching History

Directions: The purpose of this activity is to help you understand the debates over Teaching History.

Step One: To complete this activity you will need to find an article(s) that discusses both sides of the debate. You can try an internet search with "debates over teaching history" in the search box. One article that may appear in your search results is "The Debate over History's Role in Teaching Citizenship and Patriotism," a report commissioned by the Organization of American Historians. This article can be retrieved at the following URL address: **www.oah.org/reports/tradhist.html#Anchor-4716**

Step Two: Read the article(s) you found, or the one cited above, and then complete the T-chart on the opposite page. Some arguments you should address in your T-chart include the following:

- ☐ The purpose of teaching history

- ☐ Students' knowledge of history

- ☐ Teachers' knowledge of history/teacher training

- ☐ Discussion of need for state standards and/or what state standards should contain

- ☐ Curriculum issues: core curriculum; "dumbing" down the curriculum

- ☐ Terms like presentism, revisionism, multiculturalism, global education

- ☐ Solutions offered by each side of the debate

You should also record the names of people on both sides of the debate as well as their positions or job titles.

The Debates over Teaching History T-Chart

Proponents of Traditional History	Opponents of Traditional History

Two Approaches for Teaching Social Studies

Directions: The purpose of this activity is to help you understand the debates about teaching history versus teaching social studies. Descriptors that relate to each approach as well as arguments for each one appear below. Your task will be to write the descriptors and arguments in their correct positions on the Venn Diagram on the opposite page. (Hint: three items will be included in the "Both" category and four items will be placed in each of the other categories.)

◇ **Advanced Placement Exams encourage high school teachers to focus on single subjects**

◇ **Better able to analyze social, economic, and political issues faced by global society with this approach**

◇ **Best to study a topic from the perspective of many academic disciplines**

◇ **Essential for students to learn the important content and methods of research used by scholars in the field**

◇ **Goal is to develop informed, responsible, and active citizens**

◇ **History is emphasized; other disciplines are not given equal time**

◇ **Includes content from history, geography, economics, political science, and the behavioral sciences (psychology, anthropology, and sociology)**

◇ **Integrated and multidisciplinary**

◇ **NAEP (National Assessment of Education Progress) cites several examples of students' lack of knowledge in history, geography, and civics**

◇ **Separate standards created for history, geography, economics, and civics have led to this approach**

◇ **Stress improvement can be made in the teaching of all social sciences**

Two Approaches Venn Diagram

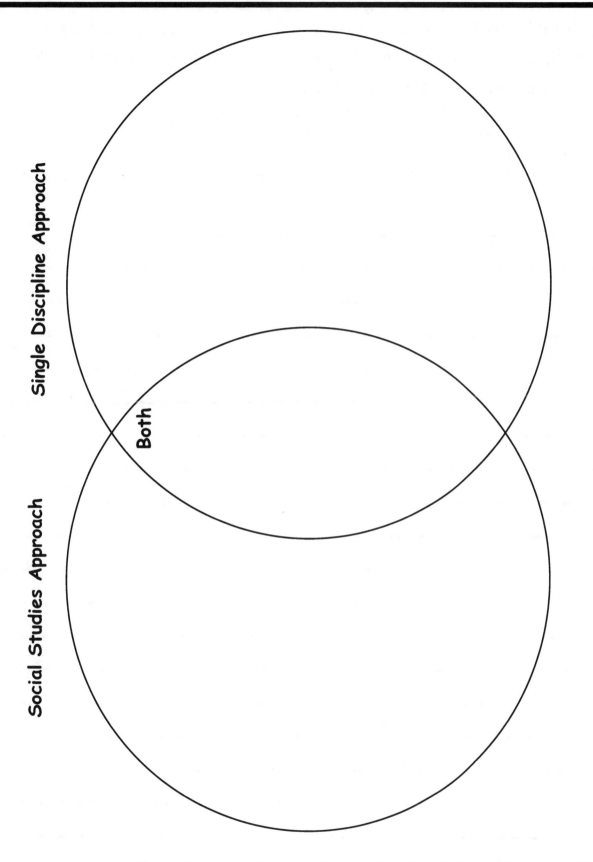

Single Discipline Approach

Both

Social Studies Approach

Where do YOU Stand on the Issues?

Directions: Where do you stand on the issues raised in the "Debates over Teaching History" and/or "Two Approaches for Teaching Social Studies" activities?

Write a 1-2 page essay in which you discuss...
- the purpose of teaching history (or social studies)
- what should be taught; (e.g., according to the standards, etc.)
- the qualifications of teachers
- which approach you'll take: single discipline? social studies? combination of both?

_____

_____

_____

_____

_____

_____

_____

_____

_____

_____

_____

_____

_____

_____

_____

_____

_____

_____

_____

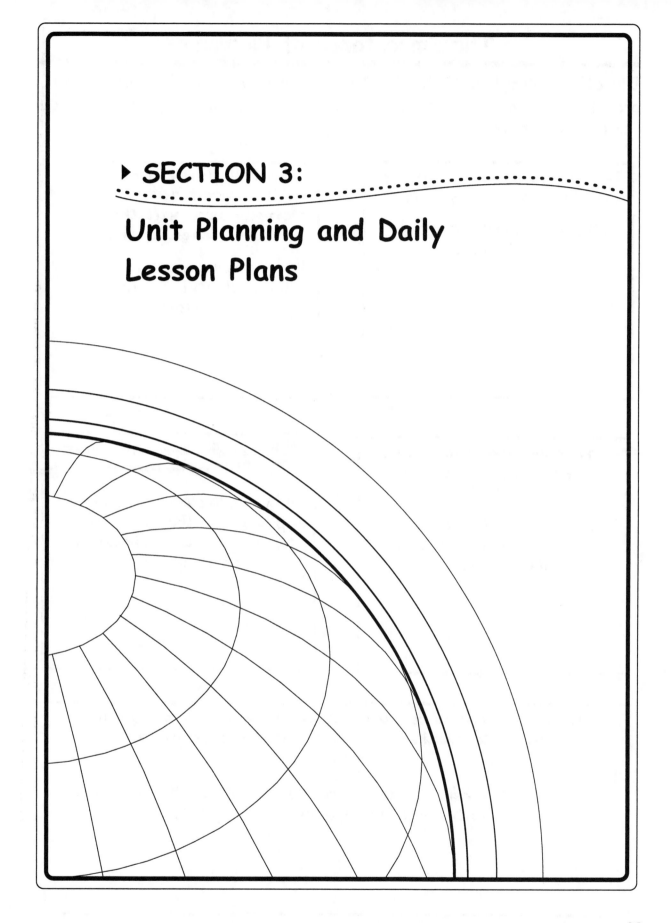

▸ SECTION 3:

Unit Planning and Daily Lesson Plans

The Importance of Planning

Directions: Complete this "graffiti" brainstorming activity by responding to the prompts written on each of the mini-posters. Record as many responses as you can think of for each prompt.

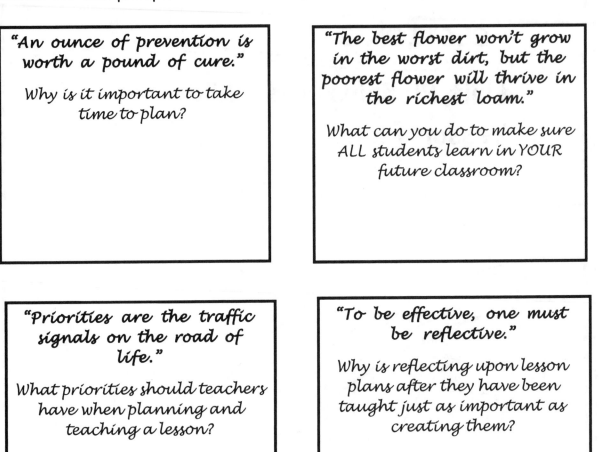

"An ounce of prevention is worth a pound of cure."

Why is it important to take time to plan?

"The best flower won't grow in the worst dirt, but the poorest flower will thrive in the richest loam."

What can you do to make sure ALL students learn in YOUR future classroom?

"Priorities are the traffic signals on the road of life."

What priorities should teachers have when planning and teaching a lesson?

"To be effective, one must be reflective."

Why is reflecting upon lesson plans after they have been taught just as important as creating them?

Albert Einstein once said, "It is the supreme art of the teacher to awaken joy in creative expression and knowledge."

Where can teachers get ideas to create lesson plans that awaken students' creative expression and knowledge?

Word Splash: How to Plan a Unit

Directions: Using <u>all</u> of the words "splashed" below, write a paragraph that demonstrates what you already know about how to plan a unit.

block schedule   inclusive classroom

assessment

objectives   unit

aligned

content   activities

integrated   standards

daily   *long-range planning*

_____

_____

_____

_____

_____

_____

_____

_____

_____

_____

_____

_____

Steps for Successful Unit Planning

Unit: a major subdivision of a course involving planned instruction around a central theme, topic, issue or problem for a period of several days or a couple of weeks.

Unit Planning: developing a sequence of daily plans that addresses the topic of a unit in cohesive way.

Directions:

Step One: Arrange the following RANDOM steps in the order you think YOU will follow when planning a unit. Write the steps on the graphic organizer that appears on the opposite page.

- ☐ Gather and prepare the materials needed for instruction.
- ☐ Look at the standards that will be addressed in the unit.
- ☐ Outline or Organize the content of the unit.
- ☐ Plan a sequence of daily lessons with appropriate instructional activities.
- ☐ Plan and prepare how students will be assessed throughout the unit.
- ☐ Select the overall goals for the unit.
- ☐ Select the topic of the unit.
- ☐ State the rationale or purpose for the unit.

Step Two: Write a brief paragraph that explains your unit planning sequence.

_____

_____

_____

_____

_____

_____

_____

_____

Steps for Successful Unit Planning Sequence Chart

Start Here: ⟶
Rearrange the steps listed on the opposite page in the order you think you will follow when planning a unit.

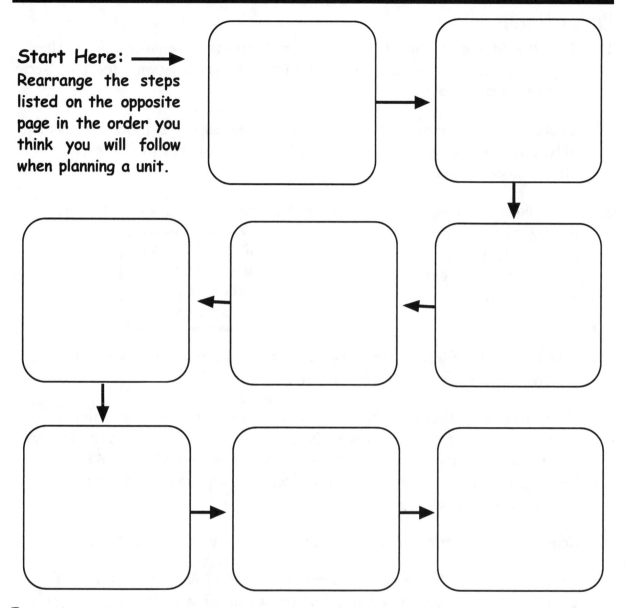

Extension: Research Grant Wiggins and Jay McTighe's backward design for planning units. Does your unit plan sequence follow their design or the traditional design? Explain.

Which planning design do you think is better? Explain.

Lesson Plan Internet Scavenger Hunt

Directions:

1. Surf the internet to find a variety of social studies lesson plans. Remember to put your search term within quotation marks to narrow your search: "social studies lesson plans."

2. In order for the Features Matrix activity on the opposite page to be more effective, you MUST visit EIGHT DIFFERENT websites to find social studies lesson plans.

3. You will need to find **FIVE** lesson plans from the following subject areas:
   a. American history
   b. world history
   c. civics/government
   d. geography
   e. economics

   → Put these lesson plans in your Teacher Resource Notebook.

4. The other THREE lesson plans may be from any social sciences subject area, but they MUST come from different sites.

5. Once you have gathered all EIGHT of your lesson plans, take some time to examine the elements of each one. In particular, pay attention to the format of the lesson plan; in other words, how is the lesson plan set up? What headings are used in each lesson plan: Grade level? Topic? Standards? Objectives? Procedures?

6. **Complete the Features Matrix. See directions on the next page.**

7. After completing the Features Matrix, answer the following questions:
   a. What elements appeared in most of the lesson plans you found?

   b. Of these common elements, which ones do you think should be in EVERY lesson plan? Explain your answer.

What's In a Lesson Plan? Features Matrix

Directions:

1) After finding eight lesson plans on the internet, write the titles of the lesson plans and their related subject areas in the first column of the features matrix below.

2) Write the elements (divisions/major headings) found in each lesson plan along the top of the features matrix. Some have been listed for you.

3) As you read through each of your lesson plans, put an X in the square/row that correlates to the lesson plan and the elements you find in each lesson plan. For an example of how to complete this step, see the sample *Causes of the Civil War* lesson plan below.

Lesson Plan Elements / Eight Lesson Plans	Grade Level	Stan-dards	Objec-tives	Assess-ment				
Title: Causes of Civil War Subject: U.S. History		X	X					

Writing Behavioral Objectives the Easy Way!

Directions: While different methods for writing behavioral objectives exist, the rules below offer a simple, yet effective method when planning daily lessons. Use these rules for the practice exercise on page 33.

Top Ten Rules for Writing Behavioral Objectives

1) The <u>objectives</u> should be connected to the state standards and the <u>specific content</u> of the day's lesson should be derived from the objectives. In other words, the standards, objectives, and the content/activities should be aligned.

   Example: 8th Grade Benchmark #2: The student uses a working knowledge an understanding of individuals, groups, ideas, developments, and turning points in the Civil War through the Industrial era of American history (1850-1900).

   Indicator 1: (Assessed Indicator) The student retraces events that let to sectionalism and eventually secession prior to the Civil War (i.e., Compromise of 1820, Compromise of 1850, Kansas-Nebraska Act, Dred Scott v. Sanford).

   The students will sequence the major events that led to the Civil War.

2) The objectives should reflect what the students should know and be able to do at the end of the lesson.

   Example: The students will define sectionalism.

3) The objective is measurable, which means the students should be able to demonstrate that learning has occurred in a way that the teacher can quantify.

   Example: The students will illustrate five major causes of the Civil War.

4) Action verbs, words like "recite, paraphrase, compare and contrast, and analyze," are used to help focus the objectives on <u>observable</u> behaviors. Using the Cognitive Domain of Bloom's Taxonomy can be helpful when selecting action verbs for your behavioral objectives. (See page 32.)

   Example: The students will compare and contrast the Compromise of 1820 and the Compromise of 1850.

5) Words like "learn," "know," and "understand" are passive verbs that should NOT be used in a behavioral objective because they are not measurable.

   Wrong: The students will understand the causes of the Civil War. (How does the teacher "know" the students understand? How can he or she measure "understand?")

6) State each objective in terms of student performance rather than teacher performance.

   Wrong: The teacher will explain the Dred Scott Decision.

   Correct: The students will summarize the Dred Scott Decision.

7) Do not state objectives in terms of a learning activity.

   Wrong: The students will get into cooperative learning groups to study the Kansas-Nebraska Act.

   Correct: The students will identify the provisions of the Kansas-Nebraska Act.

8) Objectives should be clear and brief.

   Wrong: The students will use the Cornell system of taking notes to record information about the Battle of Fort Sumter during an interactive slide lecture.

   Correct: The students will discuss the Battle of Fort Sumter.

9) State only one objective or outcome in each behavioral objective.

   Wrong: The students will compare and contrast the leadership styles of Lincoln and Davis and then write an essay.

   Correct: The students will compare and contrast Lincoln and Davis.
   Correct: The students will describe the leadership qualities of Lincoln and Davis in an essay.

10) Do not include trivial objectives.

   Wrong: The students will watch the movie Glory.

   Correct: The students will explain the hardships faced by the 54th Massachusetts Volunteer Infantry.

Bloom's Taxonomy at a Glance

Use the verbs below to help you write behavioral objectives for the Practice Exercise on the next page as well as your daily lesson plans. Please note that many of these verbs could be used at other levels on Bloom's Taxonomy. Therefore, you should make sure that the verb you select matches the intent/purpose of your behavioral objective and that it aligns with the standards, activities, and assessments you have listed in your lesson plan.

Level 1: Knowledge (gathering information)	**Useful Verbs:** identify, label, list, name, quote, recall, recognize, state, match, define, locate, recite, tell, describe, show, tabulate
Level 2: Comprehension (confirming information)	**Useful Verbs:** summarize, interpret, predict, associate, distinguish, estimate, differentiate, discuss, extend, explain, paraphrase, illustrate, give examples, rewrite, demonstrate, outline
Level 3: Application (using information)	**Useful Verbs:** compute, demonstrate, modify, practice, prepare, produce, apply, construct, plan, utilize, build, develop, organize, solve, use, act out, role play, draw, reconstruct, measure, calculate
Level 4: Analysis (breaking down or taking apart)	**Useful Verbs:** analyze, separate, order, connect, classify, arrange, divide, compare, contrast, infer, categorize, examine, subdivide, verify
Level 5: Synthesis (combining or putting together)	**Useful Verbs:** combine, create, mix, incorporate, formulate, integrate, modify, produce, collect, construct, organize, reorganize, develop, arrange, rearrange, substitute, compose, invent, rewrite, prepare, generalize, relate, design, assemble, hypothesize, assemble, imagine, originate, propose, theorize, modify, adapt, change
Level 6: Evaluation (assessing or judging results)	**Useful Verbs:** critique, decide, evaluate, support, defend, estimate, judge, appraise, predict, value, attack, score, assess, recommend, select, choose, rate, prioritize, rank, argue, grade, test, measure, convince, conclude, criticize, discriminate, justify, interpret, prioritize

Writing Behavioral Objectives Practice Exercise

Directions:

1) Look at your state's social studies standards and select a topic for which you can write a set of objectives.

2) Create two objectives for each level of Bloom's taxonomy. Be sure to consult the list of verbs in the Bloom's Taxonomy chart.

Topic of Unit: _____

Knowledge

1.

2.

Comprehension

1.

2.

Application

1.

2.

Analysis

1.

2.

Synthesis

1.

2.

Evaluation

1.

2.

How to Align Standards, Objectives, Activities and Assessments

Step One: Identify the standard and any benchmark(s) and indicator(s).

Grade 8: Civics-Government Standard: The student uses a working knowledge and understanding of governmental systems of the United States and other nations with an emphasis on the U.S. Constitution, the necessity for the rule of law, the civic values of the American republican government, and the rights, privileges, and responsibilities to become active participants in the democratic process.

Benchmark 2: The student understands the shared ideals and the diversity of American society and political culture.

Indicator 1: The student defines the rights guaranteed, granted and protected by the state and federal constitution and the amendments including the Bill of Rights.

Step Two: Write your behavioral objective(s)*.
The students will illustrate the six purposes of the government listed in the Preamble to the U.S. Constitution.

Step Three: Create the Activity(ies)*:
1.   As a class look at the Preamble of the U.S. Constitution and list on the board the six purposes listed for setting up the new government.

2.   Divide the class into six groups. Assign one purpose to each group.   Each group will create a poster that illustrates the purpose they've been assigned. The poster should include the phrase from the Preamble being identified and a picture that illustrates the purpose. When everyone is finished, each group will present their poster to the class and discuss its meaning.

Step Four: Identify the assessments that will be used to measure whether or not your students have achieved the objective(s)*.
1.   Students will have a chart with the 6 purposes listed on them. They will take notes as each group presents.   The charts will be picked up and graded. (Example of formative assessment)

2.   Students will be required to match the 6 purposes of the government to their correct description on the chapter test. (Example of a summative assessment).

*If you follow the "backward design" procedure advocated by Wiggins and McTighe, you will look at the standards and then create your assessment(s) first; next you will write your objectives and activities to match the standards and assessment(s).

Alignment Practice Exercise

Directions:

1) For each of the sample Social Studies Standards and their accompanying benchmarks and indicators provided below, you will need to create the following:

    a. One behavioral objective that will help your students meet this standard's benchmark/indicator.

    b. One activity that will help your students achieve the benchmark/indicator.

    c. One assessment that will help you determine if your students have achieved your objectives and met the standard.

2) Be sure to follow the steps on page 34.

Problem #1: Standard/Benchmark:

Civics-Government Standard: The student uses a working knowledge and understanding of governmental systems of the United States and other nations with an emphasis on the U.S. Constitution, the necessity for the rule of law, the civic values of the American republican government, and the rights, privileges, and responsibilities to become active participants in the democratic process.

3: The student understands how the U.S. Constitution allocates and restricts power and responsibility in the government.

3.3: The student compares the steps of how a bill becomes a law at state and national levels.

Objective:

Activity(ies):

Assessment(s):

****

Problem #2: Standard/Benchmark:

Grade 11 Geography: The student uses a working knowledge and understanding of the spatial organization of Earth's surface and relationships among people, places, and physical and human environments in order to explain the interactions that occur in our interconnected world.

3.1   Maps and Location: The student uses maps, graphic representations, tools, and technologies to locate, use, and present information about people, places, and environments.

Objective:

Activity(ies):

Assessment(s):

What's Wrong with the Beginning of this Class?

Directions: Read the classroom scenario (aka as a problematic situation) below and then answer the two questions that follow the scenario.

The bell rings, but not all of the students in Ms. Doe's freshman history class are in their seats ready to learn. A few are standing in the back of the room, some walk in tardy, and a few more are gathered around Ms. Doe's desk trying to find out what make-up work they need to do. The rest of the class is settled in their desks, but most are talking to their neighbors. Noting all the noise in the room, Ms. Doe yells at the students to please take their seats and for everyone to get quiet and start reading Chapter 2, Section 1 on page 35. Reluctantly, the students head to their seats; most of the students open up their books and start reading while a few others stare off into space or start talking quietly to their neighbors. After being threatened with detentions if they didn't stop talking and start reading, all students finally quiet down and either start to read or pretend to read. Ms. Doe goes to her desk and starts grading a set of papers. Every once in awhile she looks up to make sure all students are reading. After fifteen minutes of silent reading, Ms. Doe starts the day's lesson by asking a simple recall question from the reading assignment. No one raises a hand. Ms. Doe asks another simple question, but still no one raises a hand. Getting frustrated, Ms. Doe tells the students to go back and read the section again!

1) What problems can you identify in Ms. Doe's history class?

_____

_____

_____

_____

_____

2) What solutions do you have for the problems you identified above?

_____

_____

_____

_____

_____

Beginning Class Activities

What problems did you identify in Question 1 of the Problematic Situation activity on the preceding page? If you wrote that the teacher needed to begin class with some kind of an activity that would focus students' attention on the day's lesson, you have correctly identified an important element of lesson planning: a beginning class activity, also known as an anticipatory set.

Directions: To learn more about Beginning Class Activities, use the word bank below to complete the following sentences.

activating	activity	attention	engages
hooking	involve	mentally	objective
physically	purpose	overview	relevance

1. **Definition of Beginning Class Activity or Anticipatory Set:**

   A brief _____ or event at the beginning of the lesson that

   effectively _____ all students' _____ and
   focuses their thoughts on the learning objective.

2. **Purpose:**
   a. To gain the students' attention by _____ them into the lesson with an engaging activity.

   b. To prepare the students _____ and _____ for a specific learning objective.

   c. To establish the _____ of the lesson.

3. **Criteria for Beginning Class Activities:**
   a. Should relate to the students' past coursework by _____ their prior knowledge.

   b. Should provide an _____ of the day's lesson and have direct

   _____ to the instructional _____, whether that objective is implied or stated in the beginning class activity or anticipatory set.

   c. Should _____ the learner!

What's Wrong with the End of this Class?

Directions: Read the classroom scenario (aka problematic situation) below and then answer the two questions that follow the scenario.

With fifteen minutes left at the end of the class period, Mr. Buck concludes his lecture on the causes of the Civil War by telling his students that they need to read Chapter 10 for tomorrow's lesson on the Battle at Fort Sumter. As students moan and groan about the reading assignment, Mr. Buck heads back to his desk where a stack of tests from the previous class awaits him. A few students obediently begin reading Chapter 10, but most of the students start chatting with their neighbors. Soon a dull roar rouses Mr. Buck from his grading, and he yells at the students to please quiet down and read. One student defiantly tells Mr. Buck that Chapter 10 is too long to read in 15 minutes and how he doesn't understand why they have to read it because Mr. Buck will just give them the information in a lecture the next day anyway. Another student starts complaining about how all they do is read the chapters, listen to lectures, and take tests over the lectures and never do anything fun in class. She wants to know why they can't just talk to their friends since there isn't much time left in class. Growing frustrated, Mr. Buck threatens the class with a pop quiz over Chapter 10 in the next class period if they don't settle down and get quiet. Not wanting a pop quiz to lower their already low grades, the students quiet down until there is one minute to go and then the students start putting their books away and line up at the doorway. When the bell finally rings, Mr. Buck hollers at them from his desk to finish reading Chapter 10 overnight or else.

1) What problems can you identify in Mr. Buck's history class?

_____

_____

_____

_____

2) What solutions do you have for the problems you identified above?

_____

_____

_____

_____

Closure Activities

Just as it is important for teachers to begin class with some type of anticipatory set, or focus activity, it is also important for teachers to end class with some type of CLOSURE activity that effectively sums up the day's lesson and learning objectives.

Directions: To learn more about Closure, use the Word Bank to complete the following sentences that provide the definition, purpose, and criteria of closure activities.

clarifying	demonstrating	end	learned
learner	objectives	planning	practice
reinforce	reviewing	teacher	wrap-up

1. **Definition of Closure:**

   A _____ activity at the end of the lesson that reminds students what

   it was they _____ (or should have learned) and assists teachers in

   _____ for the next lesson.

2. **Purpose:**

   a. To signal the _____ of a lesson.

   b. To help organize student learning by _____ and _____ the key points of a lesson.

   c. To allow students to _____ their successful engagement of the lesson.

   d. To help the teacher decide if additional _____ is needed, if the concept needs to be retaught in a different way, or if students are ready to move on to the next part of the lesson or unit.

3. **Criteria:**

   a. Should involve the _____; closure is NOT a teacher activity but the act of the learner.

   b. Should ensure that _____ are met and applied.

   c. Should _____ the major points; closure is NOT a recapitulation of the entire lesson!

   d. Should help the _____ answer the question: "did you teach what you intended to teach and did the students learn what you intended to have them learn?"

Beginning Class Activities and Closure Activities

Directions: Surf the internet to learn about the following strategies that can be used as Beginning Class Activities (BCAs) and/or Closure Activities. Complete the chart by providing a description of the activity, its Purpose, (i.e., can the strategy be used as a BCA, Closure activity, or both?), and an example of how it could be used in the social studies classroom.

Strategy	Description	Purpose	S.S. Example
Advance Organizers			
Admit/ Exit Slips			
Analogies & Metaphors			
Brainstorming			
Current Events			
Gallery Walk			
K-W-L			
Learning Logs & Journals			
PMI: Plus/Minus/ Interesting ?			
Respond to Visual Images or Music			
Role-Playing			
Think/Pair/Share			
3-2-1			
Word Association			

Developmental Activities

In between the Beginning Class activity and the Closure activity, the daily lesson plan also includes developmental activities that teachers use to help their students achieve their objective(s). To help you identify the different kinds of developmental activities, complete the following activities.

Activity A: Drawing from Personal Experiences

Think back to your middle and high school social studies classes. What activities or strategies did your teachers use to help you learn the information? For example, did your teachers lecture, show videos/DVDs, assign study guides, etc.? Write your answers below.

Activity B: Using Lesson Plans from Features Matrix Activity

Look at the lesson plans you found for the Features Matrix activity on page 29. What activities were used in those lesson plans to help students achieve the objectives?

Activity C: Surfing the Internet

Use your favorite internet search engine to discover more social studies strategies you can use in your future classroom. Be sure to type "social studies strategies" in the search box.

> # We will look at more social studies teaching methods and strategies in the next section.

Putting it All Together: Practice Lesson Plan

Directions: Using the information you've learned in this section on Unit/Lesson Planning, create your own one-day lesson on a topic of your choice. Use the template below for your lesson plan

Grade Level:

Subject Area and Topic of this plan:

Social Studies Standard(s):

Behavioral Objective(s):

Beginning Class Activity:

Developmental Activity(ies):

Closure Activity:

Assessment(s):

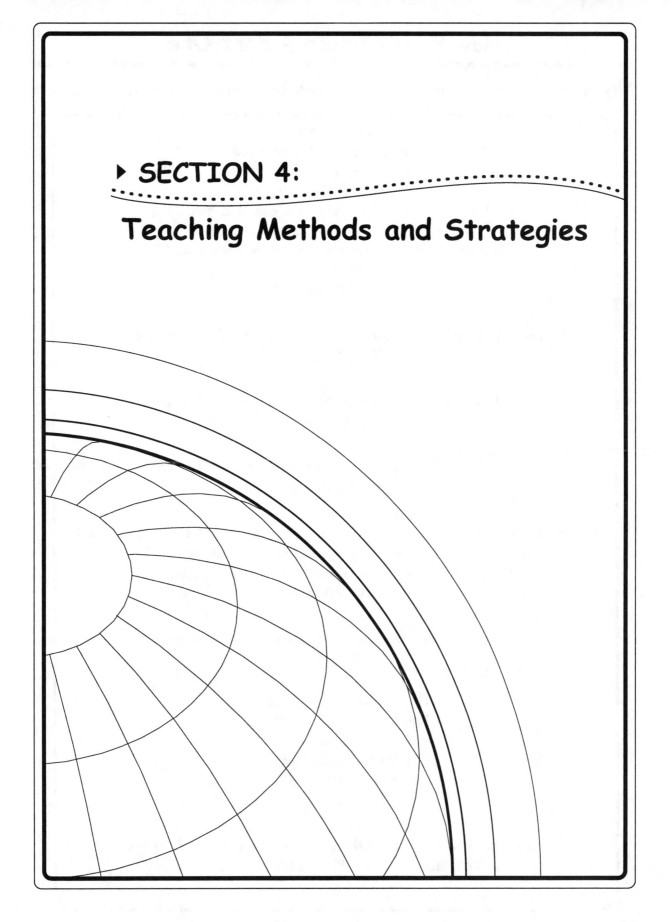

▶ **SECTION 4:**

Teaching Methods and Strategies

How People Learn - Part One

Directions: Read the following quotes to answer the questions on the next page.

"People learn...
10 percent of what they read.
20 percent of what they hear.
30 percent of what they see.
50 percent of what they both see and hear.
70 percent of what they say as they talk.
90 percent of what they teach to someone else.*"
-Eldon Ekwall and James Shanker, 1988
-*William Glasser, 1990

Thoroughly to teach another is the best way to learn for yourself.
-Tryon Edwards

By learning you will teach; by teaching you will learn.
-Latin proverb

To teach is to learn twice.
-Joseph Joubert

Don't tell them how to do it, show them how to do it and don't say a word.
If you tell them, they will watch your lips move.
If you show them, they'll want to do it themselves.
-Marie Montessori

What we have to learn to do, we learn by doing.
-Aristotle

The mediocre teacher tells.
The good teacher explains.
The superior teacher demonstrates.
The great teacher inspires.
-William Arthur Ward

Children are great mimics.
Show them how to do something and they'll want to do it too.
Tell them, and they'll sit back and watch.
-Anonymous

How People Learn - Part Two

Direction: Answer the following questions after reading the quotes on the previous page.

1) What seems to be the most effective way people learn?

2) What are some examples of teaching strategies or activities teachers could use that might be considered effective according to these quotes?

3) What are some examples of teaching strategies or activities that might be considered <u>less</u> effective?

4) How does this information fit how YOU learn best?

5) How does this information fit your vision of the teaching strategies and methods you will use in your future social studies classroom?

Three Types of Lectures

Purpose: Lecturing remains one of the common teaching methods used in a social studies classroom because it enables teachers to cover a lot of information in a short amount of time. However, critics of the lecture method often question just how much information is retained by students during a lecture. Thus, the purpose of this activity is to provide information on the different types of lectures and how you can deliver more effective lectures in your future social studies classroom.

Directions: Use print resources and/or the internet to answer the following questions. Write or type your answers to these questions on another page(s).

Part I: Formal Lectures
1. Define formal lecture.
2. What are the advantages of a formal lecture?
3. What are the disadvantages of a formal lecture?
4. What are some tips teachers should follow when...
   <u>planning</u> a formal lecture?
   <u>delivering</u> a formal lecture?

Part II: Interactive Lecture
1. Define interactive lecture.
2. What are the steps for carrying out an interactive lecture?
3. What are some examples of activities teachers can use during an interactive lecture?
4. What are the advantages and disadvantages of using the interactive lecture format?

Part III: Interactive Slide Lecture (Hint: Check out History Alive! website)
1. Describe an interactive slide lecture.
2. How is an interactive slide lecture different from a formal lecture?
   an interactive lecture?
3. What are the advantages of an interactive slide lecture?
4. What are the disadvantages of an interactive slide lecture?

Part IV: Miscellaneous Questions
1. How long do the experts say a teacher should lecture in a high school classroom?
2. How can teachers engage and/or hold students accountable for the content in a lecture?

What's Your Lecture Style?

Scenario: One of your students is at home responding to an email from a friend who missed your social studies class that day. Since you were introducing a new unit in class that day and opted to use a lecture, what will your student have to say about the "awesome" lecture you gave?

Directions: This email should be 7-10 sentences in length and should describe the type of lecture you gave that day, the topic of the lecture, and what you did during the lecture to engage your students and hold them accountable for the information.

How to Lead an Effective Class Discussion

Introduction: Think back to some of the class discussions that have been held in your high school and college classes.
a. What did you like about these class discussions?
b. What didn't you like?
c. As a future teacher, what concerns, if any, do you have about conducting class discussions in your social studies classroom?

Directions: One webpage that provides some useful tips for leading effective class discussions is "Fostering Effective Classroom Discussions" by Jennifer Barton, Paul Heilker, and David Rutkowski. Access the website and then read the information to answer the following questions. You may also wish to use other print resources and/or websites. Write or type your answers on another page(s).

www.mhhe.com/socscience/english/tc/pt/discussion/discussion.htm

1. According to this webpage, it is important for teachers to set clear expectations for student participation in a class discussion.
   a. What will you expect from your students in a class discussion?
   b. What will you do to help your students live up to your expectations?
   c. What can you have your students do before the class discussion to "prime the pump" for an effective discussion?

2. Before students will participate willingly in class discussions, they need to feel comfortable sharing their ideas with their peers and you, their teacher. What will you do to create an environment that helps your students feel comfortable sharing their ideas during a class discussion?

3. How will you arrange your classroom for a class discussion? Explain.

4. The authors of this webpage suggest that teachers "use eye contact purposefully and strategically." Why?

5. What are some examples of BAD questions you should avoid asking your students?

6. What are some examples of GOOD questions to ask your students?

7. Why should you resist responding to student comments yourself? How can you get your students to respond to each other?

Asking Effective Questions: Practice Exercise

Purpose: Part of conducting an effective classroom discussion involves asking the right questions. One strategy you can use to create good questions is to use Bloom's taxonomy as a framework for your questions.

Directions: Use the Bloom's Taxonomy chart on page 32 to help you create a set of questions you can ask on a topic of your choice.

Example:

Topic:	Battle of Gettysburg
Knowledge:	Who were the main generals involved in this battle?
Comprehension:	What mistakes were made at Gettysburg?
Application:	How could these mistakes have been corrected?
Analysis:	Why was Gettysburg considered a turning point of the Civil War?
Synthesis:	If the South had won at Gettysburg, do you think they would have won the Civil War?
Evaluation:	Should Lee be blamed for the South's loss at Gettysburg?

Your Topic: _____

Knowledge: _____

_____

Comprehension: _____

_____

Application: _____

_____

Analysis: _____

_____

Synthesis: _____

_____

Evaluation: _____

_____

Classroom Debates

Directions: A debate is a discussion in which participants justify their positions on an issue. Classroom debates can be formal or informal, depending upon the topic, grade level, length of class, and the amount of time the teacher wants to spend overall on the topic being debated. Like most common strategies, there are a multitude of internet resources that can provide information on how to conduct successful classroom debates as well many print resources. Use either type of resource to answer the questions below. (Internet search term: how to hold classroom debate) Write or type your answers on another page.

Two websites you might want to try...
www.educationworld.com/a_lesson/lesson/lesson304b.shtml
www.learnnc.org/articles/persuade-debate-0702

1. List the common steps of an informal classroom debate.

2. Why is it important to allow students time to research the topic?

3. Should students be assigned to the affirmative (pro) or negative (con) side of the debate or should they be allowed to pick which side they want to research and debate? Explain your answer.

4. What is the role of the teacher during a classroom debate?

5. What can the teacher do to ensure that the debate remains civil?

6. What are the advantages and disadvantages of using debates in the classroom?

7. Do you think you will use the debates in your classroom? Why or why not?

Socratic Seminar

Directions: If you would like to conduct a more formal whole class discussion in which your students are encouraged to have a dialogue with their peers rather than a debate, you may want to try a Socratic Seminar. Use print resources or search the internet to find websites that will help you answer the questions below*. (Search term: "Socratic seminar)

1. What is the definition of a Socratic Seminar?

2. What are the four parts of a Socratic Seminar?

3. What are the keys to conducting a successful Socratic Seminar?

4. List three differences between a dialogue and a debate.

5. How do students benefit from the Socratic Seminar method?

6. What are some tips or guidelines you can use to ensure a successful Socratic Seminar with your students?

7. Do you think you will use the Socratic Seminar in your classroom? Why or why not?

---

*For comprehensive information on how to conduct Socratic Seminars, access the Greater Rochester Teacher Center Network website:

www.greece.k12.ny.us/tlc/Socratic%20Seminars/

and download their guidebook called:

"Socratic Seminars: Creating a Community of Inquiry."

This booklet would make an excellent addition to your Teacher Resource Notebook or teaching resources file.

Structured Academic Controversy

Background: While the Socratic Seminar is for a large-group discussion, the Structured Academic Controversy (SAC) is a small-group discussion model that was developed by David W. Johnson and Roger T. Johnson.

Directions: Read the information below and then answer the questions at the bottom of the page.

Goals of SAC:
To help students... (1) gain a deeper understanding of an issue, (2) find common ground, and (3) make a decision based on evidence and logic.

Steps of the SAC Model:
1. Students are organized into groups of four, and each group is split into two pairs. One pair in a foursome studies one side of the controversy, while the second pair studies an opposing view. Partners read the background material and identify facts and arguments that support their assigned position. They prepare to advocate the position they were assigned.

2. Pairs take turns advocating their positions. Students on the other side make notes and ask questions about information they don't understand.

3. Next, pairs reverse positions. Each pair uses their notes and what they learned from the other side to make a short presentation demonstrating their understanding of the opposing view.

4. Students leave their assigned positions and discuss the issue in their foursomes, trying to find points of agreement and disagreement among group members. Teams try to reach consensus on something; if they cannot reach consensus on any substantive aspect of the issue, they should try to reach consensus on a process they could use to resolve disagreements.

5. The class debriefs the activity as a large group, focusing on how the group worked as a team and how use of the process contributed to their understanding of the issue.

Questions:
1. How does the Structured Academic Controversy (SAC) method of discussion differ from the Socratic Seminar method?

2. What are some advantages of using the SAC method? disadvantages?

3. Do you think you will use the SAC method in your classroom? Why or why not?

Recipe for a Successful Discussion

Directions: Based on what you've read about how to lead an effective discussion, how to ask good questions, and how to use different types of discussion formats, what do you think are the ingredients of a successful discussion?   Write your recipe for a successful discussion below.

Title of "recipe"

Ingredients:

Directions:

Investigating The Theory of Multiple Intelligences

Directions: Today's classroom teachers must be prepared to teach students with diverse learning styles. One way of meeting that goal is to incorporate Howard Gardner's Theory of Multiple Intelligences into the classroom. Using the Hotlist created for this assignment at the URL address below, take time to surf the websites on the Hotlist to learn more about the Theory of Multiple Intelligences and to help you answer the questions below.

www.kn.att.com/wired/fil/pages/listmidr.html#cat1

Type or write your answers to these questions on another page.

1. How does Howard Gardner define "intelligence?"

2. What are some of the key elements of Gardner's MI theory? (Hint: See Multiple Intelligences Worksheets webpage found on Hotlist.)

3. To help familiarize you with the eight intelligences commonly incorporated into classrooms, complete the Multiple Intelligences chart on the opposite page.

4. Describe two differences between traditional views of intelligence and the MI theory that you found interesting.

5. What does Gardner and other "experts" who advocate the use of MI theory in the classroom caution teachers when adapting the theory to their classrooms?

6. What are some of the criticisms of Gardner's theory?

7. What do YOU think are some of the advantages of incorporating MI into the classroom?

8. What do YOU think are some of the disadvantages of incorporating MI into the classroom?

Multiple Intelligences Chart

Directions: Use print or internet resources to complete the chart.

Intelligence	What is it?	Characteristics of Intelligence	What teachers can do to enhance Intelligence
Bodily-Kinesthetic			
Interpersonal			
Intrapersonal			
Logical-Mathematical			
Musical-Rhythmic			
Naturalist			
Verbal-Linguistic			
Visual-Spatial			

Planning a Multiple Intelligences Unit

Directions: One of the advantages of incorporating the multiple intelligences theory into the classroom is that it encourages teachers to vary their teaching strategies and activities, which in turn helps them meet the diverse needs of their students. To help you practice planning a unit that includes a variety of activities, select a social studies topic to place in the center of the MI Planning Web and then list three different activities under each of the intelligences. Please note that some activities could be placed under more than one intelligence, e.g., completing a cooperative learning activity that requires each group to illustrate one of the ten amendments could go under interpersonal, visual spatial, or bodily kinesthetic intelligences. However, for the purposes of this activity, you may only use each activity ONCE.

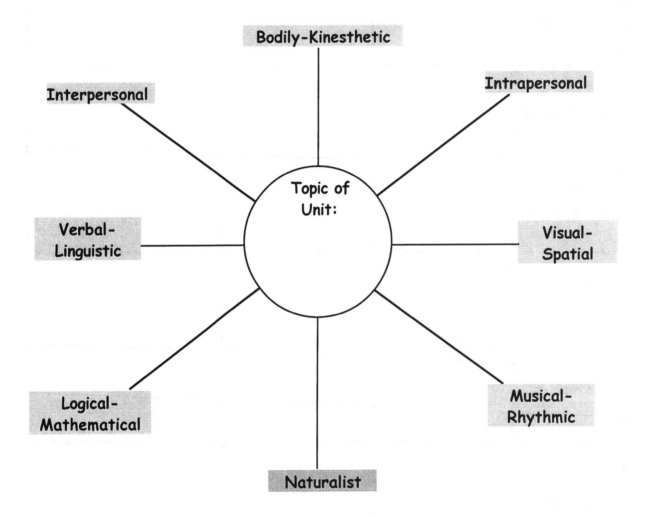

Please note that teachers are encouraged to use all eight intelligences THROUGHOUT a single unit, not all in a single day's lesson.

The Theory of Multiple Intelligences:
A Plus, Minus, Interesting Question (PMI) Activity

Directions: Based on what you have read, heard, and viewed on the Theory of Multiple Intelligences, what did you find to be a plus (P), a minus (M), or an interesting (I) question or comment? Use the following sentence stems to help you get started.*

Plus

I agree with the main ideas for the following reasons...

This fits in with what I already know about...

This has given me further insight into the situation in the following way...

Minus

I do not agree with this for the following reasons...

This is at odds with what I know about...

I have questions or concerns about...

Interesting Questions/Comments

This is a whole new slant on the subject in terms of...

I have never thought of it as...

I can adapt some of these ideas and use them by...

*adapted from *Designing Brain Compatible Learning* by Terence Parry and Gayle Gregory, 2003

What's Your Experience with Cooperative Learning?

Directions: Often the personal experiences people have had in their K-12 and college courses color their view of the methods they will choose to use in their own classrooms. One of the methodologies that is sometimes met with mixed reviews is cooperative learning. To examine your experiences with cooperative learning, complete the fishbone (cause and effect) diagrams below by listing the characteristics of your positive and negative cooperative learning experiences on the slanted lines of the fishbone. The effects have already been filled in for you.

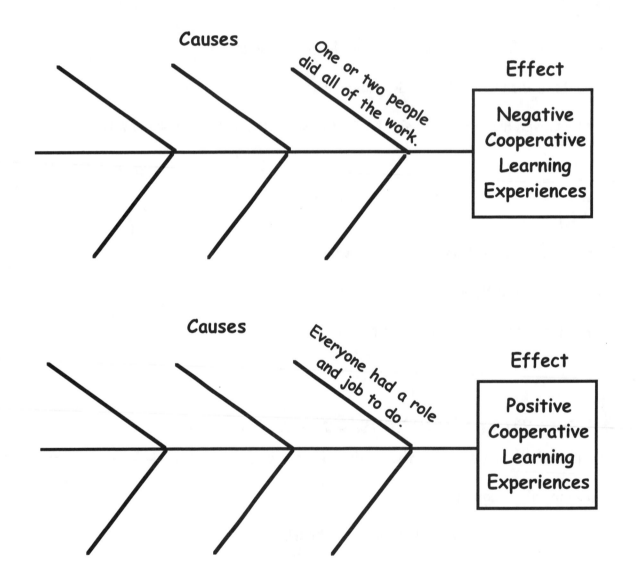

Causes

One or two people did all of the work.

Effect

Negative Cooperative Learning Experiences

Causes

Everyone had a role and job to do.

Effect

Positive Cooperative Learning Experiences

Cooperative Learning Groups or Group Work?

Chances are the negative experiences you encountered with cooperative learning were because your teachers were using "group work" and not "cooperative learning." **What is cooperative learning?** Johnson and Johnson describe cooperative learning as *teamwork within small groups of heterogeneous students working in a structured setting, with assigned roles, and towards a common goal.*

Directions: Using the definition above as well as your prior knowledge about cooperative learning, read through the list of phrases below and decide which ones describe traditional groups and which ones describe cooperative learning groups. If the phrase describes traditional groups write a capital T on the blank; if the phrase describes cooperative learning groups, write a capital C on the blank.

_____Responsibility only for oneself
_____Responsibility for each other

_____No Interdependence (Each student looks out for himself)
_____Positive Interdependence (All for one; one for all)

_____Individual Accountability
_____No Individual Accountability

_____Social skills are taught and reinforced
_____Social skills assumed

_____Students are the major source of information
_____Teacher is primary source of information

_____Teacher Interacts
_____Teacher Intervenes

_____Shared Leadership
_____One appointed Leader

_____No group processing
_____Effective group processing to discuss how the group worked together

Question: What are the major differences between traditional groups and cooperative learning groups?

Cooperative Learning Internet Scavenger Hunt

Directions: To help you complete the activities on cooperative learning and to add resources to your Teacher Resource Notebook, surf the internet to find articles on the following topics:

⬦ **Classbuilding**

⬦ **Teambuilding**

⬦ **Jigsaw Model by Aronson**

⬦ **Learning Together Cooperative Learning Model by Johnson and Johnson**

⬦ **Kagan Cooperative Learning Structures Model by Spencer Kagan**

⬦ **Articles on Kagan Cooperative Learning Structures**

⬦ **STAD and TGT Cooperative Learning Models by Slavin**

⬦ **Roles for Cooperative Learning Group Members**

⬦ **"How to" tips on...**

⬦ forming groups

⬦ managing groups and/or keeping groups on task

⬦ teaching social/collaborative skills

⬦ **Advantages and Disadvantages of Cooperative Learning**

⬦ **Using Group Grades to Evaluate Cooperative Learning Activities**

⬦ **Checklists for Teacher Evaluations of groups**

⬦ **Self-Evaluation Checklists completed by Groups**

⬦ **Cooperative Learning Lesson Plans**

⬦ **Miscellaneous Cooperative Learning articles that interest you**

Investigating Cooperative Learning Models

Directions: Use print or internet resources to research the four cooperative learning models listed in the chart below.

Founder & Model	Brief Description	Key Principles
Aronson Jigsaw		
Johnson & Johnson Learning Together		
Kagan Cooperative Learning Structures		
Slavin STAD & TGT		

Check Your Cooperative Learning IQ

Directions: Match the following Cooperative Learning Models and their basic elements to the correct description or definition. Write the letter on the blank.

_____ 1. Based on six key elements and the PIES principles: Individual Accountability, Equal Participation, and Simultaneous Interaction

_____ 2. Emphasizes team goals and team success and includes either quizzes or tournaments

_____ 3. Based on five elements that include Positive Interdependence, Face-to-Face Interaction, Individual and Group Accountability, Interpersonal Skills, and Group Processing

_____ 4. Students are assigned individual topics to teach to the other group members

_____ 5. In order for a learning situation to be cooperative, each member of the group must rely on each other to reach a common goal.

_____ 6. Each member of the group is held responsible for his/her contribution to the academic task and his/her own learning.

_____ 7. This occurs when all students are working or participating at the same time in their cooperative groups.

_____ 8. All students do the same amount of work as their group members so one person doesn't do more or less of the work.

_____ 9. Students work in close proximity to each other in a positive way, which helps build an academic and a personal support system for each member.

_____ 10. These provide students with the essential tools they need to make their groups function better and to help them be successful outside of the classroom and later in the work force.

_____ 11. The act of teachers and students discussing how well the students and their groups accomplished both the academic and social tasks in the cooperative learning activity.

A. Aronson Jigsaw

B. Equal participation

C. Face-to-Face Interaction

D. Group Processing

E. Individual Accountability

F. Johnson & Johnson "Learning Together"

G. Kagan Cooperative Learning Structures

H. Positive Interdependence

I. Simultaneous Interaction

J. Slavin's STAD & TGT

K. Social Skills

Which Cooperative Learning Models Will You Use?

Directions: Based on the information you read about the four cooperative learning models, which one(s) do you like the best and/or see yourself using the most in your future classroom? Create a visual of that frequency by creating a pie chart that shows the percentage of the time you think you will use them. Below your chart, write a brief paragraph that explains your choices.

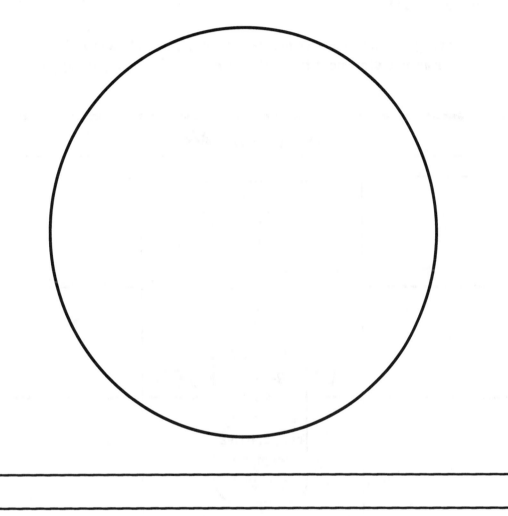

_____

_____

_____

_____

_____

_____

_____

Group Grades - Yay or Nay?

Directions:

1) Find an article(s) that discusses how to grade students in cooperative learning activities. In particular, you may want to read the opposing views of Johnson and Johnson and Spencer Kagan. One article that you may want to access on the internet is "Group Grades" by Susan Ludlow. This article presents both sides of the debate on using group grades.

2) After reading your article(s), complete the discussion web below. Don't forget to write the summary statement that reflects how you feel about using group grades.

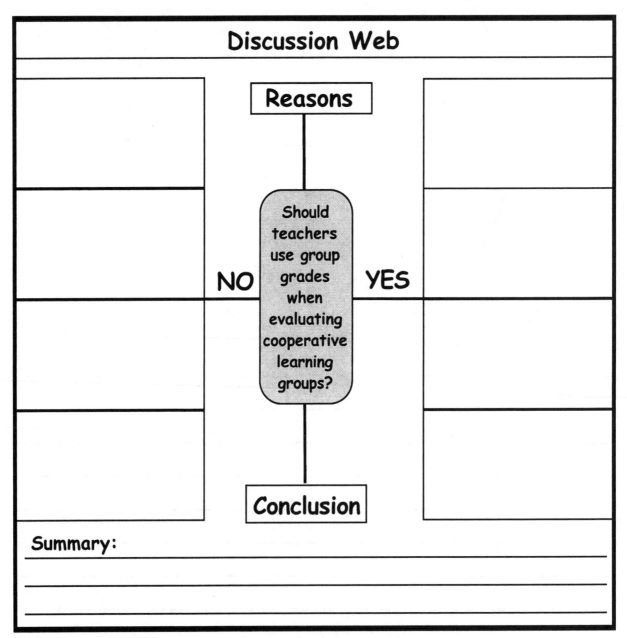

Discussion Web

Reasons

Should teachers use group grades when evaluating cooperative learning groups?

NO   YES

Conclusion

Summary:
_____

_____

_____

The Advantages and Disadvantages
of Cooperative Learning

Directions: Use print resources and the internet to find articles that discuss the advantages and disadvantages of using cooperative learning. Record the advantages on the rays of the sunshine wheel and the disadvantages inside the circle of the sun.

Summary Question: Do the advantages of cooperative learning outweigh the disadvantages? Explain.

Planning a Cooperative Learning Lesson

Directions: Use the template below to practice creating a cooperative learning lesson based on the principles of cooperative learning.

1) **Topic/Grade Level**

2) **National/State/District Standards**

3) **Purpose of Cooperative Learning Activity:**
By the end of this activity, what should students <u>know</u> and be able to <u>do</u>?

4) **Decisions to be Made Prior to Cooperative Learning Activity:**
   a. **Academic task(s):** What academic task(s) will be completed during this activity?

   b. **Social/Collaborative Skill(s):**
      1. What social/collaborative skill will be emphasized during this activity?
      2. How will this skill be introduced, monitored, and evaluated?

   c. **Group Formation:** How many members will be in each group? How will groups be formed?

   d **Positive Interdependence:** How will you foster positive interdependence?

   e. **Simultaneous Interaction:** What will you do to ensure that the majority of students are engaged at any given time?

   f. **Equal Participation:** How equal is the participation in this activity?

   g. **Face-to-face Interaction:** How is it reinforced in this activity?

   h. **Resources:** What resources will be needed to complete this activity?

5) **Directions for conducting Cooperative Learning Activity:**
   a. **Introduction:** How will you introduce this activity to your students?

   b. **Procedures:** <u>Briefly</u> outline the procedures/steps the students will follow to complete the activity.

   c. **Closure:** How will you conclude this activity with your students?

6) **Accountability/Assessment:**
   a. **Individual Accountability:** How will students be held individually accountable for the information they were supposed to learn in this activity? How will you assess this?

   b. **Group Accountability:** How will students be held accountable as a group for successfully completing the activity and learning the information? How will you assess this? Explain your choice(s).

7) **Group Processing/Debriefing:** What will you have the students do after the task is completed to debrief or process their collaborative behaviors and social skills? Explain your choice(s).

Role Playing in the Social Studies Classroom

Background: In role playing, participants adopt characters, or parts, that have personalities, motivations, and backgrounds different from their own. In the process, they can learn valuable social studies skills such as developing empathy and seeing situations from multiple perspectives.

Directions: Using internet or print resources, complete the graphic organizer below with information about role playing. Adjust the number of squares as needed; in other words, you may not use all of the squares provided or you may need to add more in some of the categories.

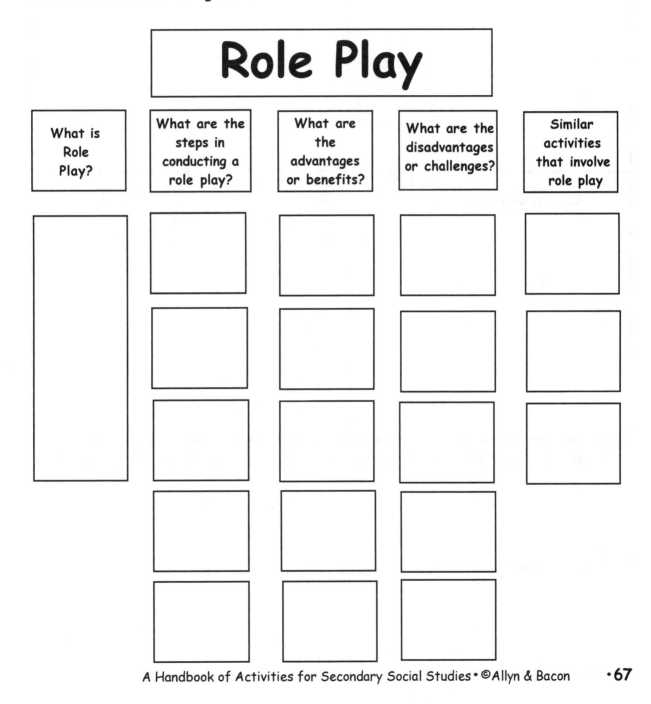

Role Play

What is Role Play?	What are the steps in conducting a role play?	What are the advantages or benefits?	What are the disadvantages or challenges?	Similar activities that involve role play

Simulations

Directions: Simulations are another example of activities social studies teachers can use to actively engage their students in the learning process. Using print or internet resources, complete the (modified) Frayer Model diagram below.

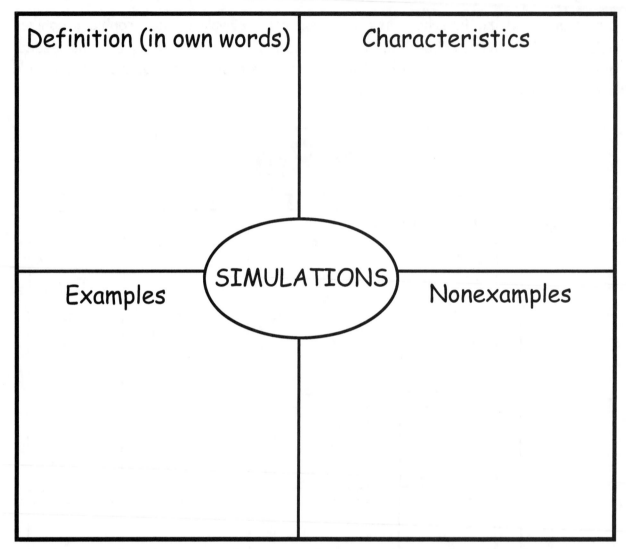

Definition (in own words)	Characteristics
Examples	Nonexamples

SIMULATIONS

1.   What are the advantages of using simulations in the social studies classroom?

2.   What are the disadvantages of using simulations?

▸ SECTION 5:

Assessment

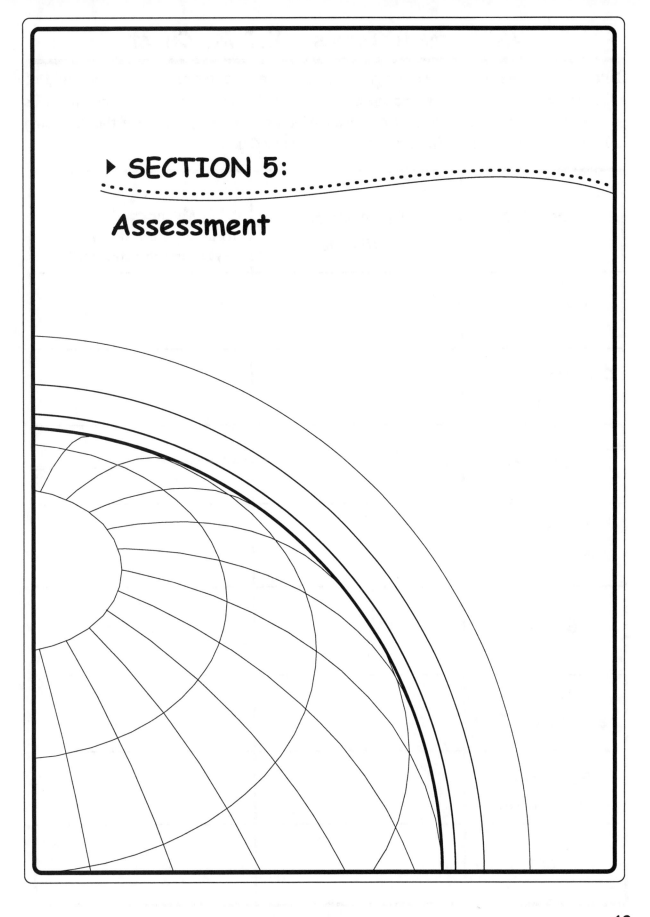

Assessment Terms: K.I.M. Chart

Directions: As you may have already discovered, the terms used in the field of education are often used interchangeably. To help you understand common terms used when discussing assessment and evaluation of students, complete the following K. I. M. chart (Key Ideas, Information, and Memory Clue).

K Key Idea	I Information (definition)	M Memory Clue (Draw a picture that will help you remember the word.)
Assessment		
Criterion-based Test		
Evaluation		
Formative Assessment		
Grades		
Norm-referenced Test		
Summative Assessment		
Test		

Assessment Role-Playing Activity

How do the stakeholders in today's world of No Child Left Behind and its mandated assessments and Adequate Yearly Progress Reports feel about assessment and tests in general? Complete the following role-playing activity to find out.

Directions: Assume the role of each group identified in the card and think about how each group might feel about local, state, and national assessments. For example, what's at stake for each group? What are the advantages and disadvantages of assessment? Also, try to look at viewpoints from each end of the spectrum for the identified groups. Write down comments they might say in the boxes provided. To get you started, a few comments have been recorded in a couple of the boxes.

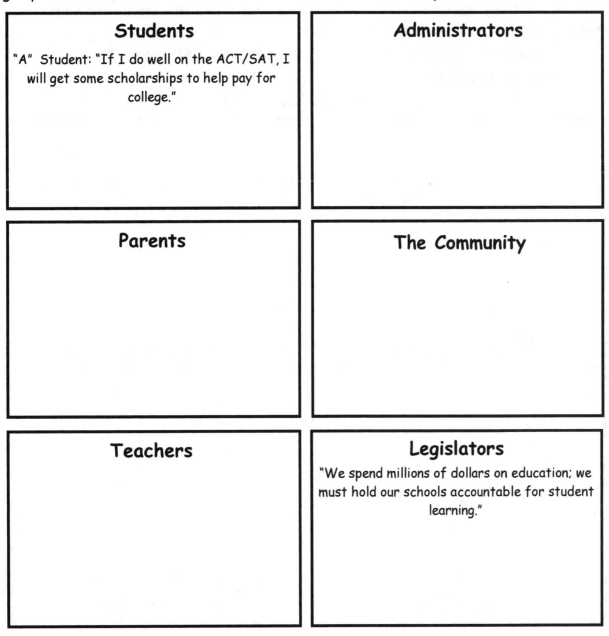

Students

"A" Student: "If I do well on the ACT/SAT, I will get some scholarships to help pay for college."

Administrators

Parents

The Community

Teachers

Legislators

"We spend millions of dollars on education; we must hold our schools accountable for student learning."

Traditional vs Authentic Assessment
Vocabulary Terms

Directions: Two more terms that you should be familiar with as a beginning teacher are "Traditional Assessment" and Authentic Assessment." To learn the difference between these two terms as well as other terms and information associated with each type of assessment, access Jonathan Mueller's website "Authentic Assessment Toolbox" to complete the following activities.

jonathan.mueller.faculty.noctrl.edu/toolbox/index.htm

Activity #1: Verbal and Visual Word Association*

For each of the following terms, create a mini-poster like the one illustrated below. (*adapted from *Teaching Reading in Social Studies* by Doty, et al, 2003)

Traditional Assessment	Authentic Assessment
Alternative Assessment	Direct Assessment

Performance Assessment

Vocabulary Term	Visual Representation
Definition	Personal Association or Characteristics

Traditional versus Authentic Assessment: What's the Difference?

Activity #2: Read the "What is Authentic Assessment" section of Jonathan Mueller's website to answer the questions below.

jonathan.mueller.faculty.noctrl.edu/toolbox/index.htm

1. What belief or mission does Mueller say is behind both traditional and authentic assessment?

2. How does curriculum drive assessment in the traditional assessment model?

3. How does assessment drive curriculum in the authentic assessment model?

4. Does Mueller believe teachers have to choose between traditional or authentic assessment? Explain.

5. How do you feel about traditional versus authentic assessment? Do you believe there is a place for both in YOUR future classroom? Explain.

Attributes of Traditional and Authentic Assessment

Activity #3: Read "Defining Attributes of Traditional and Authentic Assessment" section of Jonathan Mueller's website to complete the Comparison Chart below. To complete the chart, just fill in each side with information that describes the headings provided.

jonathan.mueller.faculty.noctrl.edu/toolbox/whatisit.htm#similar

Traditional Assessment	Authentic Assessment
Types of Tasks	
Students select responses to show understanding.	Students perform a task to demonstrate learning.
Teacher vs Student-Structured	
Meaningful Evidence of Learning	
Teaching to the Test	

Examples of Authentic Assessment

Directions: Use the internet or print resources to find examples of the three types of authentic assessments that Jonathan Mueller describes on his "Authentic Assessment Toolbox" website. Add the examples to the empty "bubbles" on the concept map. You may add as many bubbles as you need.

jonathan.mueller.faculty.noctrl.edu/toolbox/index.htm

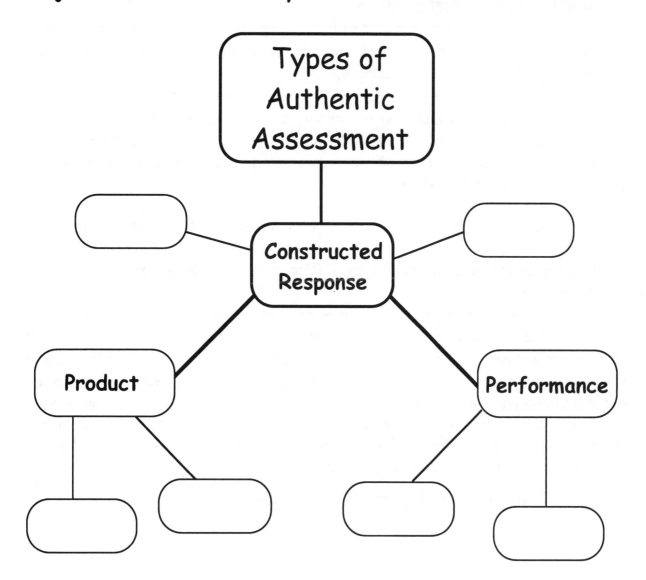

Constructing Objective Test Questions

Background: Think of the worst test you ever took. What about the test made it difficult for you? For example, were the test questions worded in such a way that you were positive the instructor was trying to trick you? To prevent your own students from feeling frustrated when they take the tests you will be creating someday, surf the internet or find print resources that offer guidelines for constructing objective test questions.

Activity #1: Complete the chart on the next page with information about constructing objective Test Questions.

Activity #2: After completing the chart, answer the following questions.

1. Which guidelines for writing objective test questions did you find the most important, especially in light of your answers to the question above about what made past tests difficult for you?

2. Which objective test questions do you think you will use the most? Explain.

3. Which websites were the most useful? (Hopefully you bookmarked them or ran off their how-to-booklets!)

Activity #3: While it can be argued that essay questions are not objective test items because they require a constructed response from students (rather than a selected response) and because there is no one correct answer, essay questions are often included on objective tests. In order for you to be able to write good essay questions, take some time to examine print or internet resources to discover how to write a good essay question. After conducting your research, write down the Top Five Tips for writing a good essay question below.

Top Five Tips for Writing Essay Questions
1.

2.

3.

4.

5.

Constructing Objective Test Questions Chart Activity

Type of Test Question	Advantages	Disadvantages	Use when you want to...	Important Tips
Fill-in-the Blank				
Matching				
Multiple Choice				
True or False?				

Using Portfolios, Rubrics, and Checklists to Assess Students

Directions: If you plan to use authentic assessments in your classroom, you will need to decide how you wish to assess your students' oral or written performances and products/projects. Three methods of assessing authentic tasks are portfolios, rubrics, and checklists. Naturally, there are different types and methods of constructing these types of assessments, so take some time to explore print or internet resources to answer the following questions.

Portfolios:

1. What are the different types/purposes of STUDENT portfolios?

2. What are the advantages and disadvantages of using portfolios?

3. What are some methods of assessing portfolios?

4. Do you think you will use portfolios in your classroom? Why or why not?

Rubrics:

1. What is a holistic rubric? An analytical rubric?

2. What are the advantages and disadvantages of using rubrics?

3. What are the steps in creating a rubric?

4. For what types of tasks do you think you will use rubrics in your classroom?

Checklists:

1. What are some situations in which checklists might be used to assess students?

2. What are the advantages and disadvantages of using checklists?

3. When might you use checklists in your classroom?

Using Multiple Measures to Assess Students

Background: Assessment "experts" warn that it is not fair to evaluate students on the basis of one single type of assessment, especially a single test score. Instead they suggest that teachers should "triangulate" their data when assessing students. In other words, every student's final grade should be based on at least three types of assessments. As a future classroom teacher, which three types of assessments do you think you will rely on to provide an accurate evaluation of your students?

Directions:

1. Label each corner of the triangle with a type of assessment you will use in your classroom on a regular basis. (Suggestions: objective tests, essay tests, oral and written projects/performances, formative assessments (daily work), portfolios, checklists, rubrics, etc.)

2. Beneath the triangle, write a brief paragraph that explains why you chose each type of assessment.

_____

_____

_____

_____

_____

_____

Assessment Activities

Activity #1: Assessment Internet Scavenger Hunt

Surf the internet to find information about the following assessment topics. Add them to your Teacher Resource Notebook when finished.

Authentic Assessments

Examples of Project Assessments

Examples of Performance Assessments

Student Portfolios

Rubrics

Rubric Generators

Checklists

Traditional Assessments

How to Write Multiple Choice Questions

How to Write Matching Questions

How to Write True/False Questions

How to Write Fill-in-the-Blank Questions

How to Write Essay Questions

Document Based Questions (DBQ)

Activity #2: Objective Test

Select a topic of your choice and then create an objective test that includes the items listed below. Be sure to follow the proper guidelines for writing GOOD test questions.

Five multiple choice questions

Five matching questions

Five True or False questions

Five Fill-in-the-blank questions

One Essay Question

Activity #3: Performance or Product Rubric

Using the how-to-article/information you found on how to create your own rubrics or a web-based rubric generator, create a rubric you could use to assess students in your classroom. You may wish to select an activity like an oral presentation or a product like a newspaper or poster. (Hint: To find a rubric generator, type "rubric generator" in the search box, or try this teacher-friendly website: rubistar.4teachers.org/index.php)

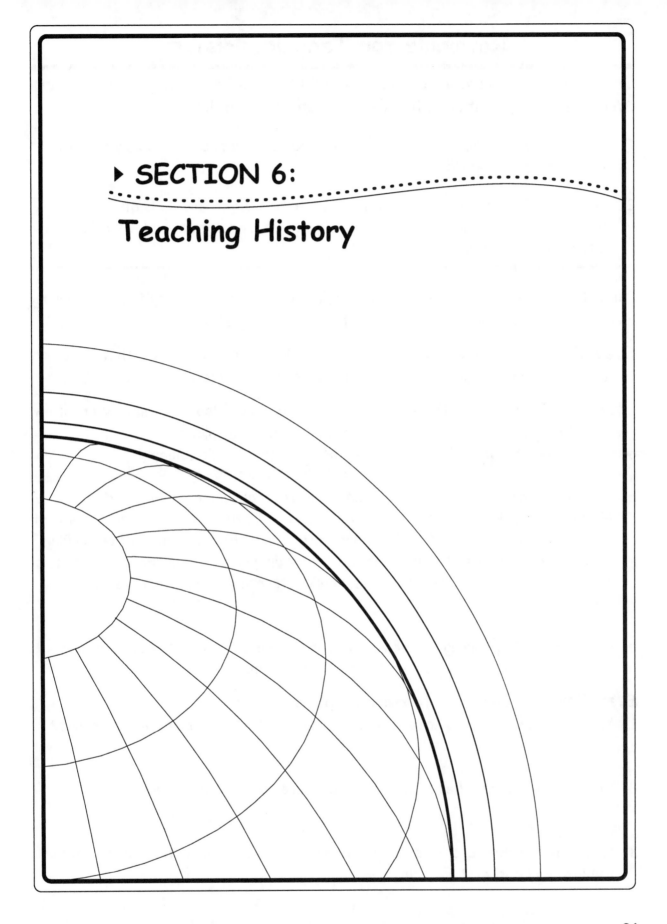

▶ SECTION 6:

Teaching History

Rationale for Teaching History

Background: According to June Chapin (*A Practical Guide to Secondary Social Studies*, 2006), the rationale for teaching history is twofold:

1) Historical Understanding: All students need to know about the history of their nation and of the world.

2) Historical Thinking Skills: Students need to be taught the skills of chronological thinking, historical analysis and interpretation, and historical research capabilities.

Directions: To help you analyze history lesson plans and identify their underlying characteristics and/or purposes, complete the following steps:

Step One: Surf the internet to find six lesson plans: three that focus on topics in American history and three that focus on world history topics.

Step Two: Complete the Features Matrix on the opposite page by carefully reading through each lesson plan. After reading the lesson plans...
a. Write the title or topic of the lesson plan in the far left column.

b. Read the characteristics of Teaching for Historical Understanding and Historical Thinking Skills listed on the matrix. If the lesson plan contains that characteristic, place an X in the appropriate block. For example, if Lesson Plan #1 uses song lyrics to teach about the Cold War, place an X in the column that states "Students can use visual arts, music, literature, etc. to understand history."

c. Continue reading through all of your lesson plans and marking the appropriate characteristics as they pertain to each lesson plan.

Step Three: Answer the following questions.
1. Which characteristics were the most common in the lesson plans you examined?

2. Why do you suppose these characteristics were the most common?

3. Which of the characteristics do you think are the most important to promote or use in the classroom? Explain.

Rationale for Teaching History Lesson Plan Activity

How many of these characteristics can be found in the lesson plans you found? Put an **X** in the appropriate squares. **Title/Topic of History LP**	Characteristics of Teaching for Historical Understanding and Historical Thinking Skills							
	Students need to understand history of their nation and world	Students can use visual arts, music, literature, etc. to understand history	View time from a larger perspective to help students get a sense of history	Promote Chronological Thinking Skills & Historical Analysis and Interpretation	Encourage students to use the methods of historians to identify and analyze current problems	Promote citizenship; develop personal identity in diverse world & empathy for others		

Resources for Teaching for Historical Understanding

Directions: Each of the items below can be used in social studies classrooms to teach for historical understanding. Create a chart like the one below and provide definitions/descriptions and examples of how to use these resources in ANY social studies classroom (not just history).

Resource	Definition/ Description/ Examples	Brief Explanation of how you would use the Resource in your social studies classroom
Art Work		
Artifacts		
Field Trips: Real or Virtual		
Jackdaws		
Journals & Magazines		
Literature		
Media		
Music		
Photos		
Posters		
Simulations		
Textbook & Resource Kit		
Videos/DVDs/ CD Roms		

Using Primary Sources to Teach Historical Thinking Skills

Background: Primary sources are one means of promoting historical thinking skills (and understanding history). To help familiarize you with the vast number of primary sources available on the internet, complete the pamphlet activity below.

Scenario: You have been asked by the State Department of Education to create a pamphlet for first-year social studies teachers on using primary sources in their classrooms.

Content

Your pamphlet must contain the following information:
- A definition/examples of primary sources
- A definition/examples of secondary sources
- Benefits of using primary sources
- Guidelines for selecting and using primary sources
- How/where to find primary sources
- Top Ten Primary Sources Websites that the busy first-year teacher can trust to have quality sources related for American and world history. Be sure to include the types of primary sources found on each website and some specific examples of each type (e.g., WWII propaganda poster; Oregon trail diary, etc.)

Design Tips:

Be sure to make your pamphlet as colorful and eye-catching as you can.
Create headings for each of the required sections.
Use fonts that are clear and easy to read.
Use graphics/clip art wisely to break up each section.
Your pamphlet should have at least "one" fold in order to look like a pamphlet.

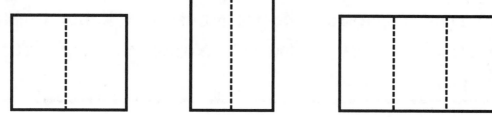

Methods for Teaching for Historical Understanding and Historical Thinking Skills

Directions: There are many teaching/learning models that social studies teachers can use to promote historical understanding and historical thinking skills. Some of these models include:

Inquiry-Based Learning (e.g., Dewey, GATHER, etc.)
Problem-Based Learning
Project-Based Learning
Thematic Learning/Interdisciplinary Units
Oral History

To learn more about these models, use print or internet resources to complete the graphic organizers on the following pages. For each model, you will need to provide:

A. a definition of the model and/or its overall purpose.

B. an explanation of how it can be implemented in the social studies classroom. Most models have a step-by-step procedure teachers/students can follow.

C. the pros and cons of using the model.

D. examples of each model and/or any miscellaneous information that will help you understand the model and/or implement the model in your future classroom.

Helpful Hint: As you research each learning model on the internet, be sure to bookmark the most useful sites and/or print copies of the web-based articles to place in your Teacher Resource Notebook for future reference.

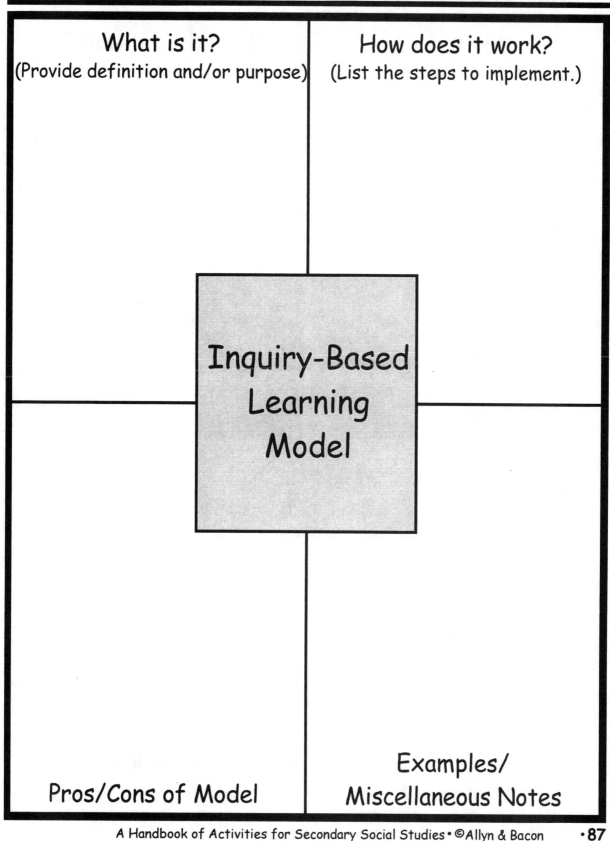

What is it?
(Provide definition and/or purpose)

How does it work?
(List the steps to implement.)

Inquiry-Based Learning Model

Pros/Cons of Model

Examples/ Miscellaneous Notes

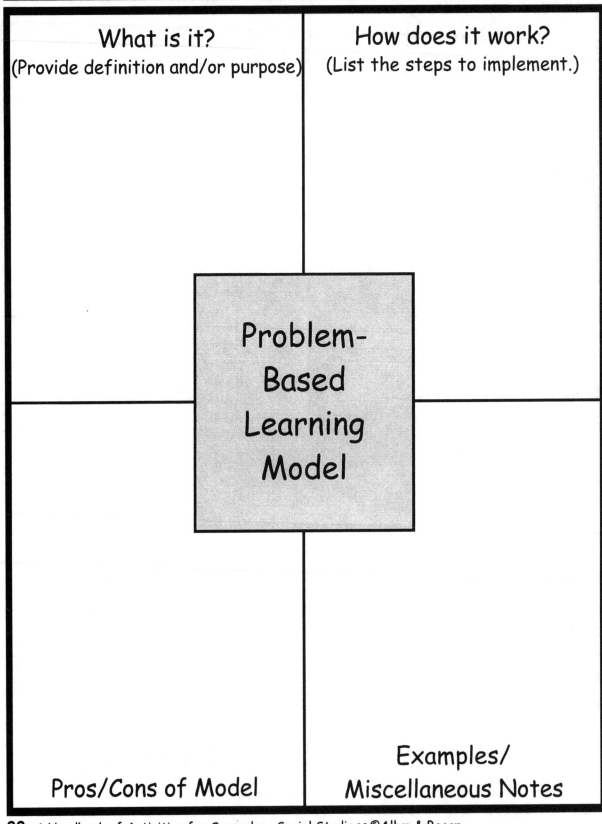

What is it?
(Provide definition and/or purpose)

How does it work?
(List the steps to implement.)

Problem-Based Learning Model

Pros/Cons of Model

Examples/ Miscellaneous Notes

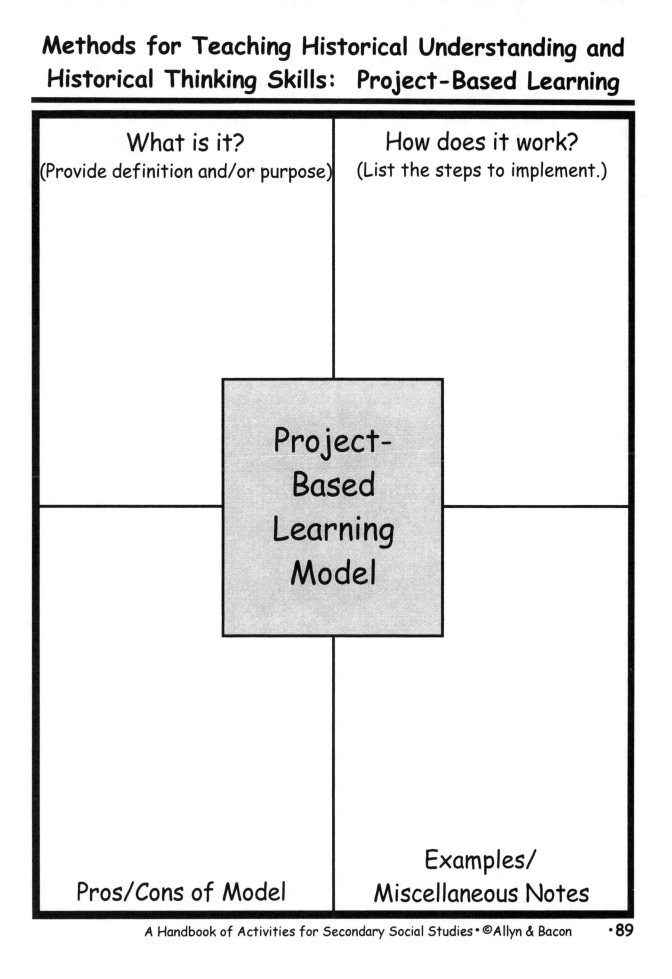

What is it?
(Provide definition and/or purpose)

How does it work?
(List the steps to implement.)

Project-Based Learning Model

Pros/Cons of Model

Examples/Miscellaneous Notes

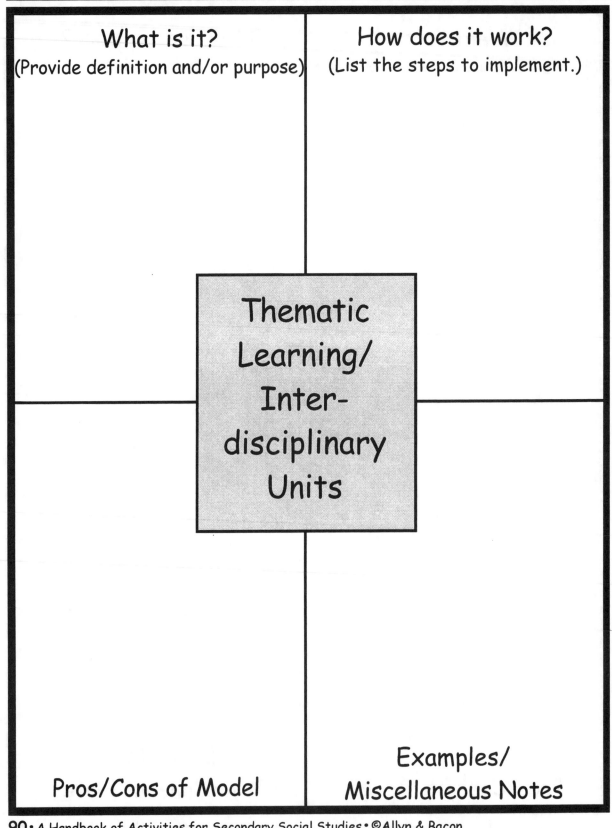

What is it?
(Provide definition and/or purpose)

How does it work?
(List the steps to implement.)

Thematic Learning/ Inter- disciplinary Units

Pros/Cons of Model

Examples/ Miscellaneous Notes

Methods for Teaching Historical Understanding and Historical Thinking Skills: Oral History

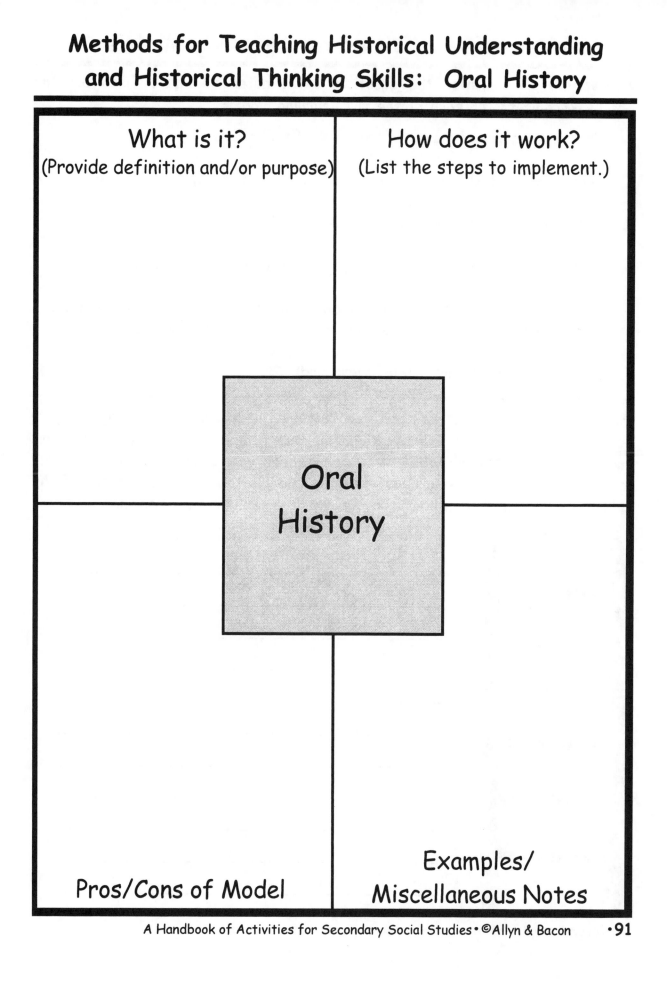

What is it?
(Provide definition and/or purpose)

How does it work?
(List the steps to implement.)

Oral History

Pros/Cons of Model

Examples/
Miscellaneous Notes

Summary Activities for Learning Models

Activity #1: Answer the questions below after you have filled out the graphic organizers for each of the five learning models.

1. What common elements can be found in all of the models?

2. Were there any major differences between the models? If so, what where they?

3. How do these models help students understand history better?

4. What historical thinking skills are being promoted in these learning models?

5. In addition to promoting historical understanding and historical thinking skills, what other benefits do students gain from the use of these models?

6. What are the drawbacks of using these models?

Activity #2: Use the ladder below to rank the learning models according to how much you think you will use them in your future social studies classroom and/or how effective you think they are. Place your favorite model(s) at the top of the ladder and your least favorite models towards the bottom of the ladder. When finished, write a paragraph that explains your rankings.

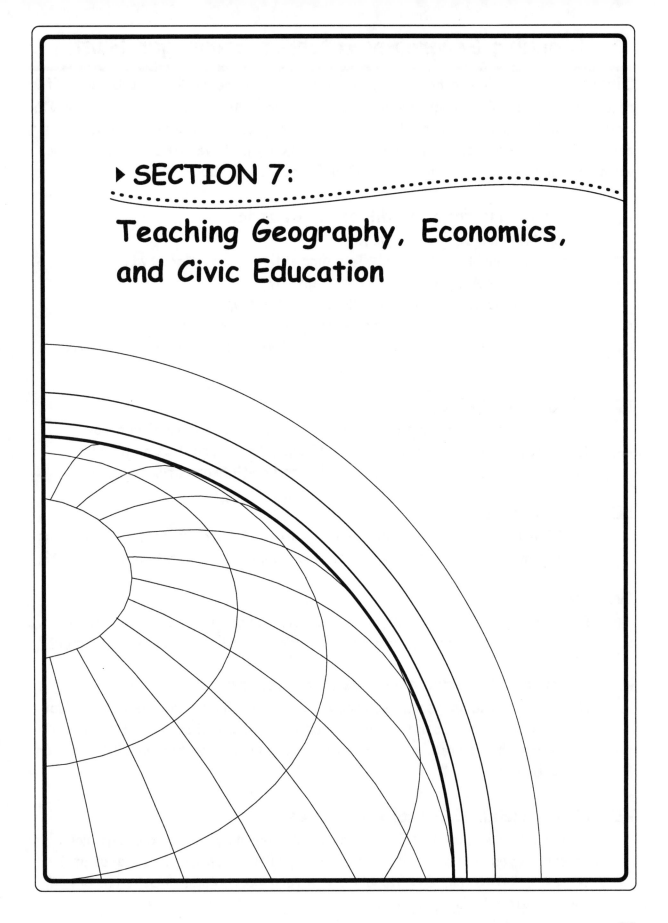

▸ **SECTION 7:**

Teaching Geography, Economics, and Civic Education

Teaching Geography Internet Scavenger Hunt

Directions: There are many excellent websites on the worldwideweb that offer resources for teaching geography in K-12 classrooms. As you look for the **TWENTY** items below, be sure to bookmark the websites on your computer as well as run off copies of the lesson plans and homepages so you will have a hard copy of these valuable resources to place in your Teacher Resource Notebook.

I. Lesson plans from six different websites
1 from National Geographic website
1 from National Park Service's Teaching with Historic Places website
1 that address ALL five themes of Geography
1 that addresses any of the five themes of Geography
2 from sites not used for the previous three lesson plans
*Try to vary the topics so you will have a variety of resources in your Teacher Resource Notebook.

II. Geography Quizzes
Find 2 websites with geography quizzes teachers can use to either make their own quizzes or can send their students to for practice or to take a Geography Quiz that is automatically scored on the computer.

III. Geography Games
Find 2 websites with geography games that will "trick" students into learning geography. Be sure to find games that will appeal to students in grades 7-12.

IV. Map Resources
Find 2 Websites which offer maps teachers can print off and use in their classroom. These kinds of maps are often referred to as "blackline masters."

V. Resources for Problem-Based/Project-Based Lessons
History isn't the only social science discipline in which students can conduct research projects. Look for three websites that would provide information for geography-related topics and projects. (Hint: Look for the CIA Facts on File webpage!)

VI. Miscellaneous Geography Websites
Look for five websites that contain useful geography resources. The more resources you find now will not only save you time later but also a lot of stress! (Hint: Include National Council for Geographic Education as one of your websites.) Happy Surfing!

NCGE's Countdown to Geographic Awareness

Directions: Increase your understanding of the importance of learning "Geography for Life" by completing the pyramid below. You can find the missing information on the National Council for Geographic Education website. The exact link is: www.ncge.org/publications/tutorial/overview/

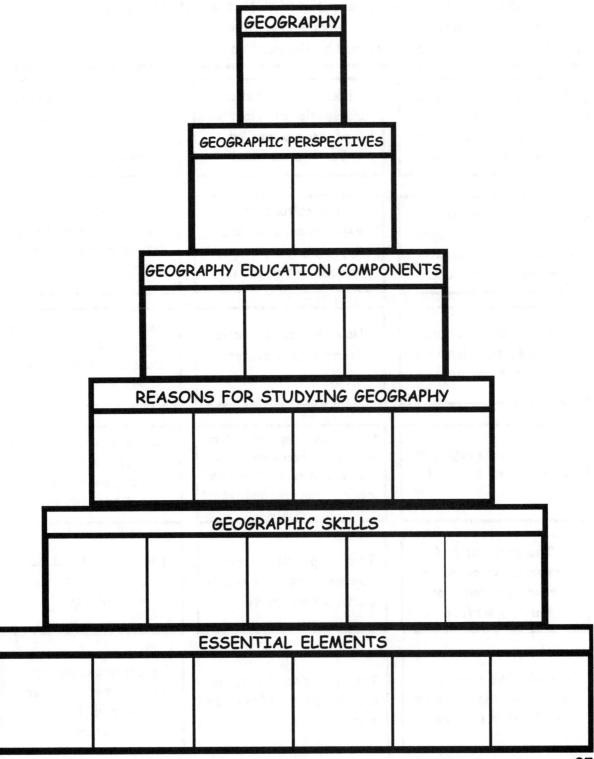

GEOGRAPHY

GEOGRAPHIC PERSPECTIVES

GEOGRAPHY EDUCATION COMPONENTS

REASONS FOR STUDYING GEOGRAPHY

GEOGRAPHIC SKILLS

ESSENTIAL ELEMENTS

Geography Standards Sorting Activity

Directions: In 1994 the National Council for Geographic Education adopted the national geography standards called "Geography for Life." These eighteen standards are organized around six essential elements: the World in Spatial Terms, Places and Regions, Physical Systems, Human Systems, Environment and Society, and the Uses of Geography. To help you get acquainted with the national geography standards, complete this sorting activity by placing the standards listed below (in alphabetical order) under their correct headings on the next page.

The changes that occur in the meaning, use, distribution, and importance of resources.	The characteristics and spatial distribution of ecosystems on Earth's surface.	The characteristics, distributions, and complexity of Earth's cultural mosaics.
The characteristics, distribution, and migration of human populations on Earth's surface.	How culture and experience influence people's perception of places and regions.	How forces of cooperation and conflict among people influence the division and control of Earth's surface.
How human actions modify the physical environment.	How physical systems affect human systems.	How to analyze the spatial organization of people, places, and environments on Earth's surface.
How to apply geography to interpret the past.	How to use maps and other geographic representations, tools, and technologies to acquire, process, and report information.	How to use mental maps to organize information about people, places, and environments.
The patterns and networks of economic interdependence on Earth's surface.	That people create regions to interpret Earth's complexity.	The physical and human characteristics of places.
The physical processes that shape the patterns of Earth's surface.	The process, patterns, and functions of human settlement.	To apply geography to interpret the present and plan for the future.

Geography Standards Sorting Activity

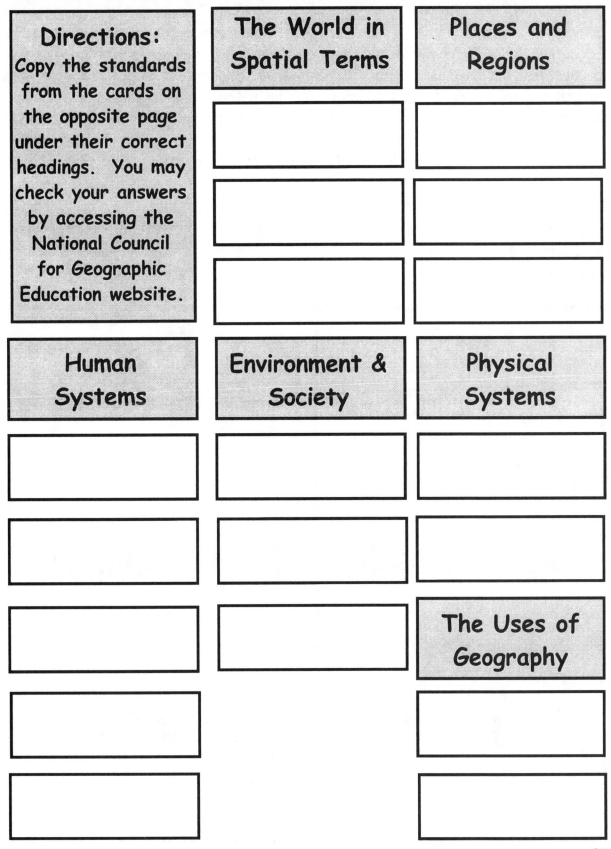

Directions: Copy the standards from the cards on the opposite page under their correct headings. You may check your answers by accessing the National Council for Geographic Education website.

The World in Spatial Terms

Places and Regions

Human Systems

Environment & Society

Physical Systems

The Uses of Geography

Five Themes of Geography Poster Activity

Background: In 1984 the "Five themes of Geography" were written by the Joint Committee on Geographic Education of the National Council for Geographic Education (NCGE) and the Association of American Geographers (AAG). The five themes were designed as a framework upon which the content of geography could be taught, and they served the K-12 population until the national geography standards were published in 1994. Since the six elements of the national standards embrace the five themes, they remain a valuable tool for students to use in developing a "geographic perspective," while the standards strengthen instructional planning.

Directions: Create a mini-poster of each of the five themes of geography by filling in the posters with a definition of the theme, an illustration(s) that provides an example(s) of the theme, and at least one activity or strategy you could use to help your students learn each theme.

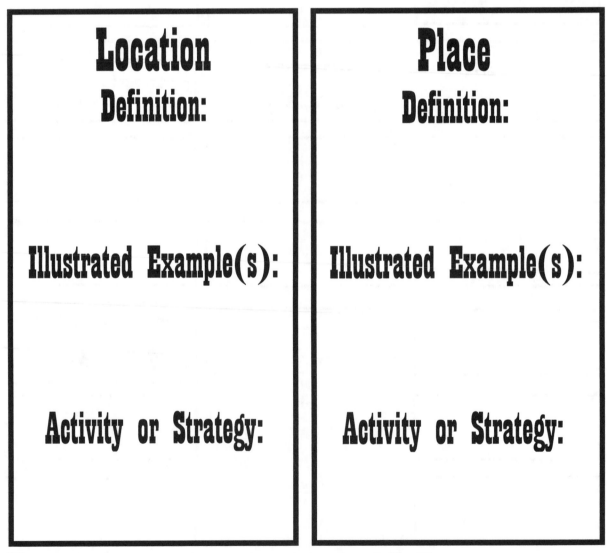

Location
Definition:

Illustrated Example(s):

Activity or Strategy:

Place
Definition:

Illustrated Example(s):

Activity or Strategy:

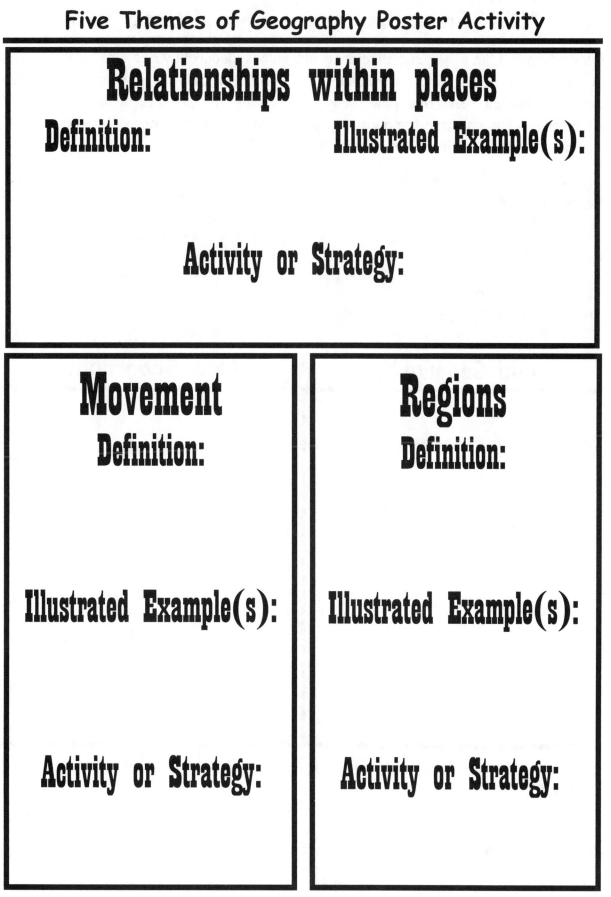

Relationships within places

Definition:

Illustrated Example(s):

Activity or Strategy:

Movement
Definition:

Illustrated Example(s):

Activity or Strategy:

Regions
Definition:

Illustrated Example(s):

Activity or Strategy:

"Old" Geography versus "New" Geography

Directions: Like other social science disciplines, geography has also made changes in the way it delivers its curriculum. The word bank below contains phrases that describe the "old" and the "new" geography. Place the phrases under the correct headings and then answer the questions at the bottom of the page. (Source: Chapin, *A Practical Guide to Secondary Social Studies*, 2006)

Adaptable to new technology
Connected to critical thinking skills
Emphasis on spatial relationships
Encourages problem solving
Framework or standards-driven
Limited problem solving and skill development
Place location memorization
Textbook-driven, with recall of information a prime goal

Collaborative learning strategies
Depth replaces breadth
Emphasis on human/environmental issues
Fact-based objective testing
Hooray! It's Field Trip Day
Observation through field work
Research-based

Old Geography	New Geography

1. Which geography is most like what you experienced in middle school or high school?

2. How might the "new" geography be better for students?

Teaching Geography Acrostic

Directions: After completing the preceding geography-related activities, create an ACROSTIC about what you've learned about teaching geography. (An acrostic uses the letters of a word spelled vertically to create horizontal sentences or phrases that relate to the vertical word.) See the example below to get you started.

G

E

O

Games can trick students into learning the location of countries and their capitals.

R

A

P

H

Y

Mirror, Mirror on the Wall, Teaching Econ is so Dismal!

1. Why do you suppose economics has the reputation of being the "dismal science?"

2. How many economics courses have you taken in both high school and college? Would you describe them as dismal? Why or why not?

3. How do YOU feel about teaching economics?

Exploring the National Council on Economic Education Website: www.ncee.net

Directions: According to the National Council on Economic Education's website, NCEE was established over 50 years ago with the goal of "establishing comprehensive programs that equip teachers with tools to get economics and personal finance into the classroom and to help students apply in their lives what they learn in school." Select four of the programs and/or tools on their website that you think will be the most beneficial to you as a beginning social studies teacher. Write the name of each resource and a brief description of the resources in the boxes below. Be sure to bookmark the links and/or make hardcopies of the resources you find for your Teacher Resource Notebook.

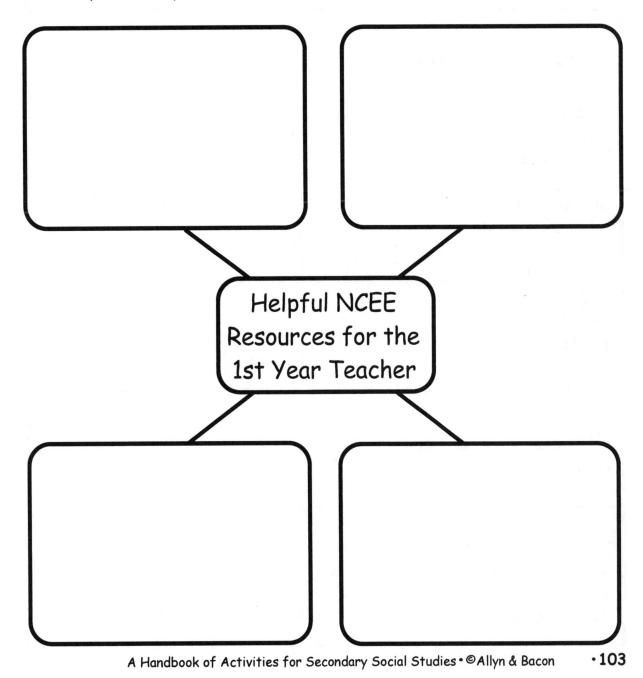

Helpful NCEE Resources for the 1st Year Teacher

Examining the National Standards for Economics

Directions: Complete the 5Ws and H graphic organizer below by accessing the National Council on Economic Education website (www.ncee.net/ea/standards/) and reading about the development of the national economics standards. While exploring the standards, be sure to print off the printer-friendly version of the standards for your Teacher Resource Notebook as well as any other resources you find.

Who wrote the national economics standards?	
What is included in each of the standards?	
When students have finished the twelfth grade, what kinds of general knowledge should they have gained?	
Where can teachers find lesson plans that support the standards?	
Why should economics be taught in grades K-12?	
How does economics improve students' reasoning skills? (List the skills that are improved.)	

Economics Lesson Plans

Directions: Like the other social science disciplines, economic lesson plans are plentiful on the internet. However, what makes a good economics lesson plan from a beginning teacher's point of view? Select two websites that offer lesson plans and spend some time exploring a variety of lesson plans that address different standards and concepts as well as ones that use different methods (like simulations and case studies). Next, complete the compare/contrast graphic organizer below with the positive and negative features of each website's lesson plans. When finished, write a summary paragraph that states which website you think is the best for beginning teachers. Be sure to run hard copies of your favorite lesson plans to place in your Teacher Resource Notebook.

Website #1:	Website #2:	Website #1:	Website #2:
Compare		**Contrast**	
Quantity		Quantity	
Variety of topics, concepts, standards addressed		Variety of topics, concepts, standards addressed	
Content of Lesson Plans		Content of Lesson Plans	
Miscellaneous		Miscellaneous	
Overall Quality		Overall Quality	

Economic Internet Resources for "One and All"

Directions: Select four economics websites (other than NCEE) that you believe have a lot to offer first-year social studies teachers. Label the numbered sections below with the names of the websites. (Be sure to include Foundation for Teaching Economics website: www.fte.org/) After exploring each of the websites, write down the resources they have in common in the "ALL" section of the graphic organizer. Write down the resources that are unique to each website in their respective spaces.

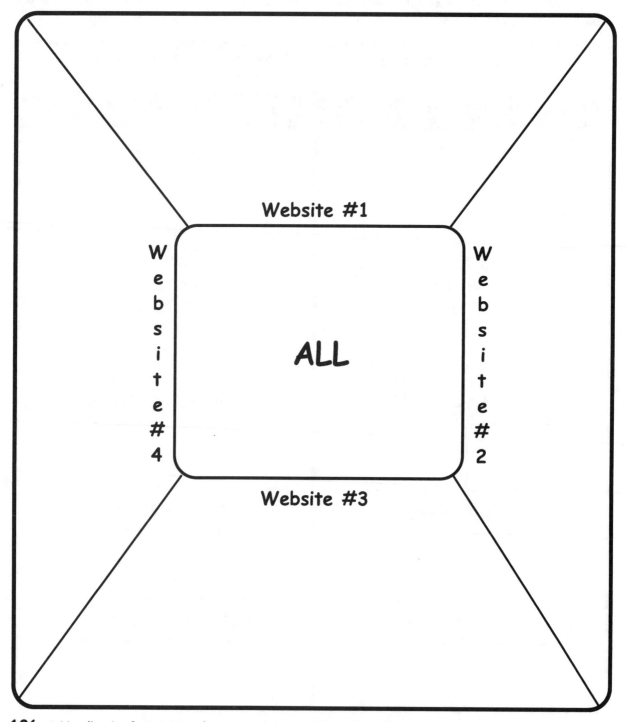

Website #1

Website #4

ALL

Website #2

Website #3

Using Simulations in the Economics Classroom

Backgrounds: Simulations are creative units of instruction that incorporate traditionally taught concepts into a simulated environment in the classroom. Often students are organized into small groups and role-play either actual persons or characterizations of persons in past, present, or future history, social, economic, or political situations. With its many real-world applications, the economics classroom is the perfect setting for simulations.

Directions: Surf the internet or use print resources to find FIVE simulations you could easily implement in your classroom. After you have selected your five simulations, complete the chart below by writing the name of the simulation and the website where you found it, the topic or economic concept being taught, and then the advantages and disadvantages of each simulation.

Name of Simulation and Website	Topic/ Economic Concept	+	−

Teaching Economics: Dismal or Enjoyable?

Now that you've completed some activities that should have acquainted you with the vast number of resources that are available to help teachers break the stereotyped image of economics as the "dismal science," what can YOU do to make economics more enjoyable for your future students? Keep your answer in mind as you complete the scenario activity below.

Scenario: In an effort to better meet the needs of its diverse students, your high school has decided to add some elective courses in the social sciences department. As the "new kid on the block," you have been asked to teach an "Everyday Economics" course for juniors and seniors. The counselors have asked you to write a course description for the course catalog. In addition to being brief, your course description must convey the overall purpose of the course as well as paint an inviting picture to entice students to enroll.   Write your course description below.

_____

_____

_____

_____

_____

_____

_____

_____

_____

_____

_____

_____

What is Civic Education?

Directions: Like many concepts and methodologies in education, there are different definitions of what civic education is. To help you develop an understanding of what Civic Education is and what it encompasses, access "The Role of Civic Education" policy paper on the Center for Civic Education's website (www.civiced.org/articles_role.html). After reading the article, type up your answers to the questions below.

1. What is civic education?

2. What are the three essential components of a good civic education?

3. What five questions should be asked to engage students in civic knowledge?

4. Give two examples of intellectual and participatory skills that students should possess.

5. What are the five essential traits/dispositions of an effective citizen?

6. Where should civic education take place?

7. Give four examples of the rights and responsibilities that formal instruction should emphasize to students (two of each).

8. Give two examples of co-curricular programs in which students are taught civic principles and ideals.

9. Give two examples of community service activities in which students can participate.

10. Why does civic education need to be taught and/or improved?

11. What is the relationship between civic education and character education?

National Standards for Civics and Government

Directions: Access the National Standards for Civics and Government at the Center for Civic Education website (www.civiced.org/stds.html). Take time to explore the standards and this section of the Center's website before completing the activities below.

Question #1: On a scale of 1-10, how appropriate are the standards created for grades 5-8 and 9-12? Mark an X on the line to represent your rating.

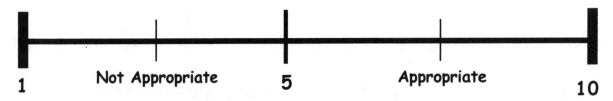

Explain your rating of the standards. In other words, what makes the standards appropriate (or not appropriate) for students in grades 5-12?

Question #2: On a scale of 1-10, how teacher-friendly is this webpage that contains the standards and information about the standards? Mark an X on the line to represent your rating.

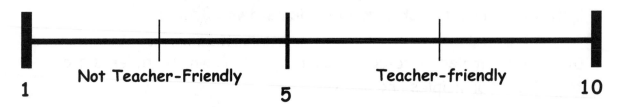

Explain your rating of the website's "friendliness" with at least three reasons or examples:

Directions: Complete the graphic organizer using print or internet resources.

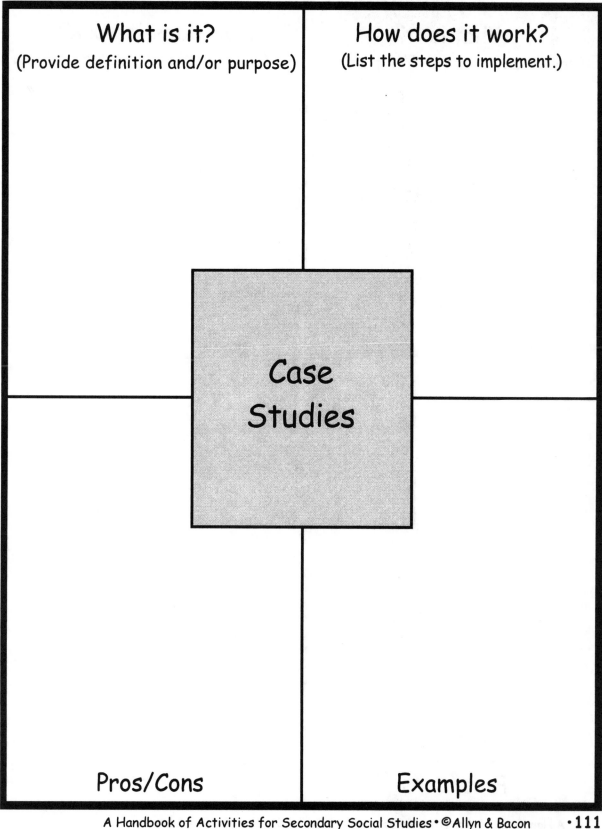

What is it?
(Provide definition and/or purpose)

How does it work?
(List the steps to implement.)

Case Studies

Pros/Cons

Examples

Directions: Complete the graphic organizer using print or internet resources.

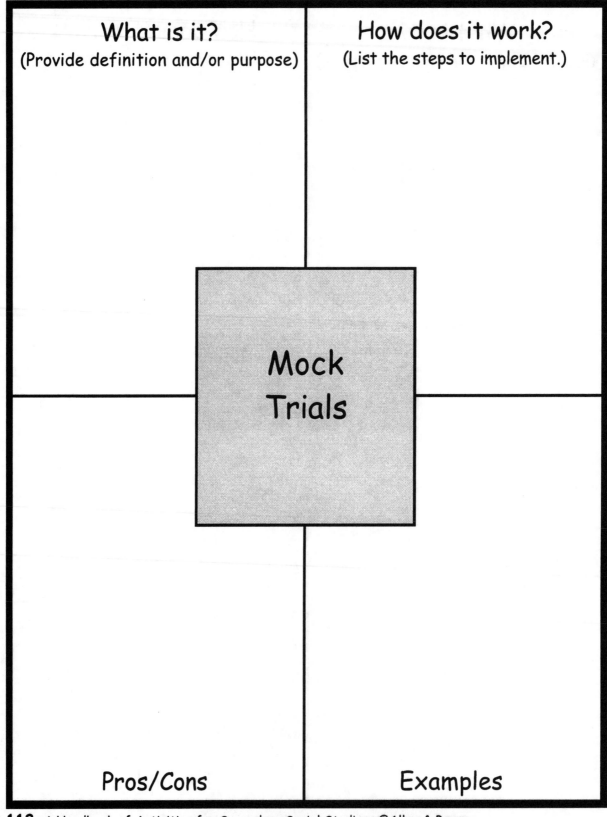

What is it?
(Provide definition and/or purpose)

How does it work?
(List the steps to implement.)

Mock
Trials

Pros/Cons

Examples

Directions: Complete the graphic organizer using print or internet resources.

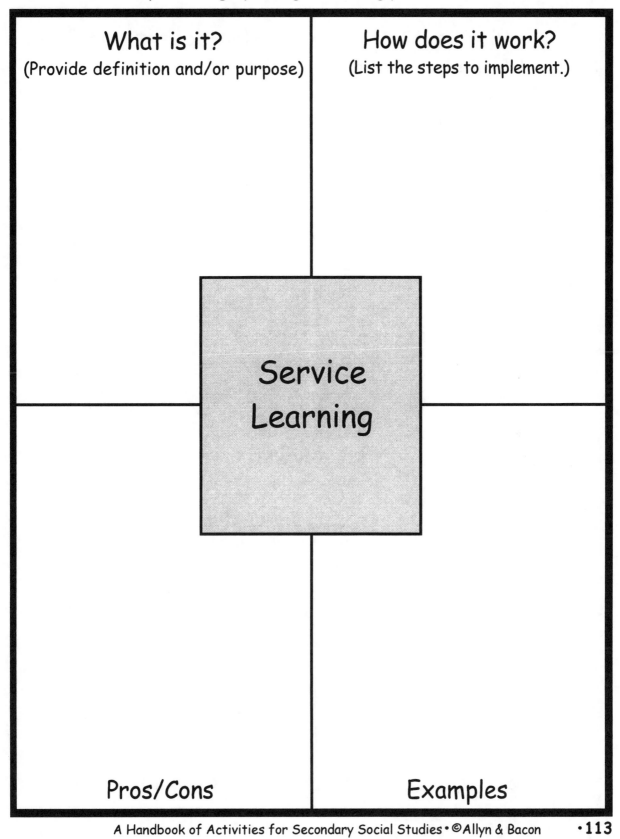

What is it?
(Provide definition and/or purpose)

How does it work?
(List the steps to implement.)

Service Learning

Pros/Cons

Examples

Methods for Teaching Civics/Gov't: Issues Approach

Directions: Complete the graphic organizer using print or internet resources.

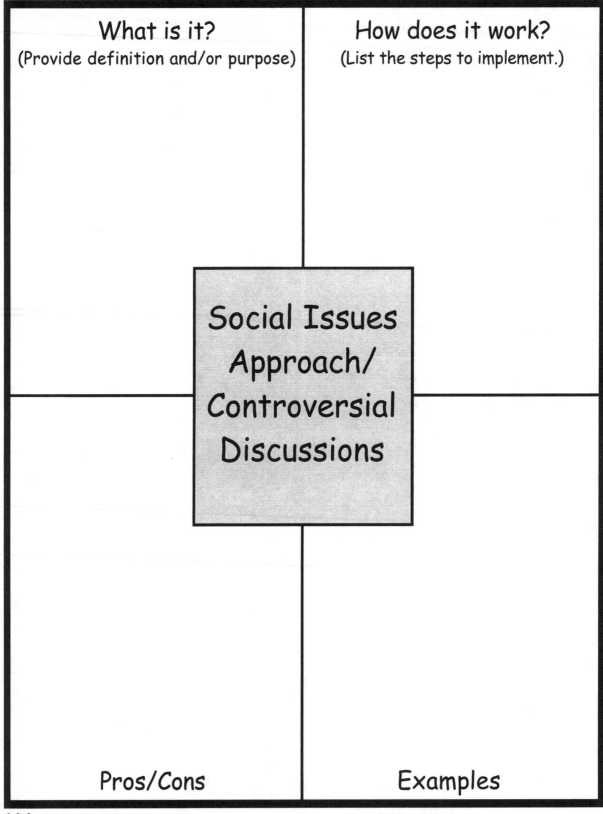

What is it?
(Provide definition and/or purpose)

How does it work?
(List the steps to implement.)

Social Issues Approach/ Controversial Discussions

Pros/Cons

Examples

How to Teach Controversial Issues

Scenario:

Recently the school in which you are teaching has received several parental complaints about their children participating in class discussions and/or projects that involve topics they believe are inappropriate for the public school classroom. Since there are no written guidelines in your district for teaching controversial issues, the principal has asked YOU to create a presentation for the next school board meeting that discusses the merits of teaching controversial issues and provides guidelines for conducting civil and appropriate class discussions. He has also asked you to create a sample project that illustrates the educational value of asking students to research a controversial topic in a formal manner. For your presentation, you will need to create a handout that you can give to parents and the media who will be attending the school board meeting.

Contents of "Teaching Controversial Issues" Handout

A.   Definition of controversial issues

B.   Reasons WHY controversial issues should be taught in the public schools and the BENEFITS of teaching controversial issues (at least three of each)

C.   Guidelines for Teaching controversial issues
   1.   Selecting controversial issues (include such things as who selects the issues and criteria for selecting issues)

   2.   The Teacher's role in teaching controversial issues (Be sure to discuss whether or not teachers should share their opinions with students.)

   3.   Tips that will help teachers conduct civil discussions on controversial topics

   4.   "Rules" for students to follow during discussions of controversial issues

D.   Examples of sample student projects and topics

What's Your Angle: Teach or Preach?

"Teacher put on leave for Bush remarks"
"Colorado teacher on leave after alleged anti-Bush remarks"

These are just two headlines that appeared in newspapers across the nation after geography teacher Jay Bennish's comments about President Bush were recorded electronically by a student during a class lecture and then aired publicly a few weeks later. This incident prompted many discussions about whether or not teachers have the right to express their personal opinions in the public school classroom, especially when discussing controversial subjects. To help you examine this issue more closely, complete the Right Angle activity below.

Directions: Using print or internet resources, find information that discusses the teacher's role in classroom discussions that involve controversial issues. You may also want to find examples of school policies that specifically state what rights teachers have when conducting discussions. You will use this factual information to answer the questions by the horizontal arrow.

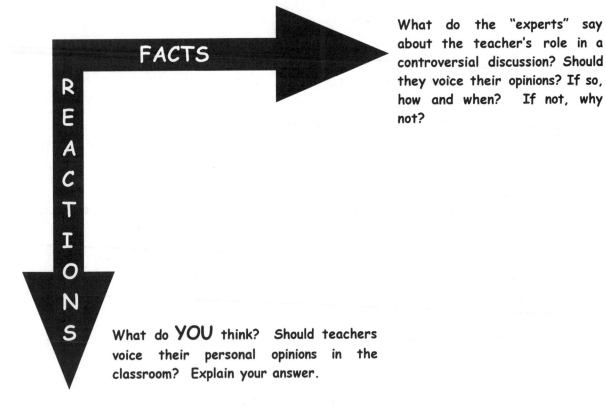

FACTS

REACTIONS

What do the "experts" say about the teacher's role in a controversial discussion? Should they voice their opinions? If so, how and when? If not, why not?

What do **YOU** think? Should teachers voice their personal opinions in the classroom? Explain your answer.

Think Globally, Act Locally

Scenario: Faced with images of starving children in Africa, homeless tsunami and quake victims in Asia, some of the students in your homeroom class want to know what they can do to help those less fortunate than they are. During the brainstorming session, one student shouts out, "we should help our own people first before we help a bunch of foreigners in some far off place."

As a future social studies teacher who may be faced with a discussion like this, how would you respond to this student?

Directions: Using print or internet resources, answer the following questions.

1. Define global education.

2. What are some of the goals of global education?

3. What resources are available for teaching global education?

4. Should global education be integrated into ALL social sciences courses? Why or why not?

5. How would you respond to the student in the scenario?

6. Brainstorm some projects you could do with students to help them "**Think Globally, Act Locally.**"

Project Ideas	Resources for carrying out the projects

Increasing Multicultural Awareness in the Classroom

Directions: Use print or internet resources to complete the 1-2-3-4 activity below. (A website you might want to access is the National Association for Multicultural Education (NAME) at www.nameorg.org).

1 Definition of Multicultural Education

2 National organizations that promote multicultural education

3 Resources for teaching multicultural education

4 Lesson Plan ideas